OPTIONS TRADING

The crash course for beginners with the best strategies for passive income. How to make money profit fast investing options and stocks. Tips and Tricks to trade for a living

Author Name:

Andrew Steve Hammer

Table of Contents

Introduction 1
Chapter 1: The Basics of Options Trading 3
    Stocks 3
        A Stock Market 4
        Why the Stock Market? 5
        How to Trade In Stocks.. 6
        Key Players in the Stock Market 7
        Various Types of Stocks 9
    Reasons Why Companies Sell Shares 11
Chapter 2: Options Trading Basics 15
    Types of Options Trading 16
        Call Option... 17
        Put Option 18
    Intrinsic value 19
    Advantages of Trading with Options........................... 20
    Options and Time 24
    Components of an Option Contract 25
    Fundamentals of Option Pricing 28
Chapter 3: How to Begin Option Trading 30
    Preparing for the Options Trade 33
    Setting off With the Trade 35
Chapter 4: Tools and Types of Trading Platforms 37
    Definition of a Trading Platform.................................. 37
    Trading Platform Basics 38
        Types of Platforms 38
    Trading Option's Features 39
    How to Select a Trading Platform 40
    Ethical Considerations for an Options Trader 42
        1. Interactive Brokers Platform............................... 44

2. Trade-Station Trading Platform 45
   3. TD-Ameri-Trade 46
   4. Robinhood Trading Platform 46
   5. Charles Schwab Platform 47
   6. Ally Trade Invest 47
   7. E-Trade 48
  Option Trading Instruments.. 48
Chapter 5: Financial leverage 52
  Definition... 52
  Why Leverage Is Referred To As a Risky Venture 53
  How Leverage Is Used For The Benefit Of the Trader 54
  Pros and Cons for Leverage Trading 55
  Trading Smarter With Options...................................... 57
     How to Trade Smarter With Leverage 62
Chapter 6: Technical Analysis.................................66
  Top-Down Technique.. 68
  Bottom-Up Technique 68
  Characteristics of Technical Analysis 70
  Technical Analysis Charts 71
     Bar Charts 72
     Line Charts 73
     Candlestick Charts... 74
     Renko Charts... 75
  Benefits of Technical Analysis 76
  How to Apply Technical Analysis................................ 78
Chapter 7: Mindset, Controlling Your Emotions (Trading Psychology)..81
  Fear.. 83
  Greed 84
  Things that Distinguish Winning and Losing Traders in Option Trading 86
  Trading Strategies.. 91
  Traps to Avoid on Expiration Day............................... 92

Chapter 8: Options Trading Strategies For Beginners 94
   Long Put 94
   Protective Put or Married put 95
   Bear Put Spread 96

Chapter 9: Stock Investing Trading Strategies for Beginners 107
   Strategies for Investing in stocks 107
      Value investing 107
      Growth Stock investment Strategy 108
      Passive Index Investing 111
   Indicators of Investing Stock Strategies 112
      Simple Moving Averages 113
      Rate of Change 114
      RSI-RELATIVE STRENGTH INDEX 115
      Moving Average Convergence Divergence 116

Chapter 10: Tips and Tricks to Trade for a Living ... 120

Chapter 11: Brokers 131
   Insurance Brokers 131
   Real Estate Broker 132
      Roles 133
   Stock Brokers 134
      Full-Service Brokers 135
      Discount brokers 135
   Roles of Stock Traders 136
   High-End Brokers 138
      Roles of High-End Brokers 139
   Online Brokers 140
      Roles of Online Brokers 140
   How to Invest with Brokers 141

Conclusion 142

Introduction

Other than the common financial instruments such as stocks and bonds, there is yet another different class of investments called derivatives. These instruments have their prices originating from underlying assets.

Options are derivatives which can be traded by investors. They offer opportunities for the purchase of underlying assets, for example, stock, at a predefined cost and date.

An option by way of definition, it is a financial instrument which is derived from and underlying security like stocks as well as bonds. Based on the type of contract you hold, you can decide to sell or purchase options at any stated value.

Options come in two distinct sets: the American and the European options. For the case of the American options, they allow you to exercise options strictly at expiration whereas European options are very flexible and therefore allow you to exercise them at any time as long as you have not reached the expiration date.

Just like any contract ever heard of, options operate in a similar way. They define various details concerning a trade. Payment is necessary for the option for you to trade in it. However, it is not a necessity.

Chapter 1: The Basics of Options Trading

Stocks

What hits your mindset whenever you hear of a stock? It is a kind of investment that depicts an owned share within a company. Therefore investors go for shares which are predestined to appreciate in their future values.

In addition to the above definition, stock can be termed as security for an ownership share in a company. There are various reasons why companies issue out stocks to the public. One of them is to raise more funds which can be used for further investment in their business.

To the investor, a share increases their monies which can be used to counter inflation with time. Those who own shares in companies are referred to as shareholders. They are thus eligible for sharing the company's proceeds.

Stocks are ever bought from companies with a primary objective that their future value will appreciate. If it so happens, the value of the stock will literally go up, which can later be sold for profit.

A Stock Market

A market, as you know, is a place where the exchange of goods and services take place. It can be in the open air, over some form of media and it includes the buyers and sellers of that which is being traded in.

This is a place where stocks are exchanged or sold by public companies. There are very many examples of *stock market exchange* across the globe like NASDAQ. This business is conducted through some form of intermediaries called stockbrokers. As the exchange goes on, there is sufficient track of the supplies and demands for every company's stocks.

In the same way, the stock market is a public platform for trading of stock. It as well, it could be over the counter or any other format. The differentiating factor is that, in this case, the variable being traded is stock or equity and not goods.

A stock is simply a small part of ownership in a certain company. If you wish to have an ownership in this company, then you will need to visit the stock market where such business takes place. Owners of the companies through the acquisition of shares are called investors.

A stock market which is booming is rated as an economic booster because it makes companies make their capital faster and more swiftly from the investors and the general public.

Why the Stock Market?

A stock market is essential to companies. Through the same, companies are able to make their capital from the potential investors who come to buy shares and others dispose of their already purchased shares to others. This capital is required to fund the company's programs.

Suppose a company is offering $10 million shares of stock to the market and each share is going for $11 per share; therefore the company will receive $110 million which it can use to increase the capital base for production. This is far much better than a bank loan or any other borrowings from other companies.

This also helps the companies avoid unnecessary debts and subsequent interests that would be paid to the respective lenders of their capital.

Another advantage goes to the investors who after buying shares of stocks will have to enjoy dividends of the profits earned. There is a ratio in which claims are issued out to potential investors. Some companies offer standard dividends per share owned, whereas some investors decide to trade-in their shares as the stock prices go up for profits.

For instance, suppose an investor bought shares initially at $12 per share, and thereafter the prices go up to $17 of the same stock, the shareholder may deem it better to dispose of his shares for a profit.

How to Trade In Stocks

Generally, stocks are traded in the exchange markets known around the globe. There are government bodies that regulate the stocks exchange. This is done to protect the investors from fraud activities that may lead to lack of trust in the business.

Even if most stocks happen on exchanges, there are those few that take place over the counter where dealers are involved in the stocks. Over the counter, stocks are those that don't meet the minimum requirements to be listed on the stock exchange.

This kind of stocks is not exposed to the same public exchange rules as for those listed. As a result, investors cannot be able to get any relevant information concerning such stocks. That's why dealers come in to act as links between the stock owners and the potential buyers.

Key Players in the Stock Market

There are various key players in trading with stocks on the stock market. They are but not limited to: Inventors, Investment Banks, and Stockbrokers.

· *Investment Banks*

This deal with what is referred to as IPO's, that is initial-public-offering of stocks which come about shortly after the decision of a company to begin to offer shares of its stocks publicly.

· *How does an investment bank offer the IPO's for the company?*

Take an example of bank q and company x. When company x decides to enter the market by offering its stock to the public in terms of shares; it will visit bank q as its choice to help them get the investors.

Bank q will, first of all, come in as the underwriter for the deal. It will do some prior evaluation of the company to establish its capital base and its liquidity. After that, they will have to agree on the payments per share offered after the selling.

The bank then goes ahead to list the shares of the stock at its cost on the exchange for investors to buy at the maximum price possible. As soon as the shares are bought, the company pays off the bank, and the deal is closed.

· *Stock Brokers*

Stockbrokers could be individuals or companies that buy stocks from their client companies at whatever price and sells them on their behalf. They are sometimes financial-advisors to the companies that offer shares for sale to the markets.

This directly influences the prices of the company's stocks. There is a constant fluctuation of the prices of the stocks across the day; however, stock owners remain optimistic that the prices will have a positive skew.

It is not so for every company or stock because the company's value may dwindle downwards or lose business absolutely. If such a thing occurs, stock investors could end up losing part or all of what they had invested.

It is, therefore, advisable for investors to have or purchase shares across various companies rather than narrowing their focus on a single company. There are various types of stocks that can be traded in as you will learn in the next subtopic.

Various Types of Stocks

There are mainly two different types which are so far known and are being practiced widely. They are preferred as well as common stocks.

1. Common Stock

As the name suggests, it is so common to almost every common stock business investor. By default, whenever one precisely talks about such investment, he could be talking about common stocks without his prior knowledge. Most stocks are ever offered in this way.

This is when someone has ownership of shares in any given company and is entitled to dividends of profits in a certain ratio. Board membership is elected by the shareholders. Each shareholder has got only one vote to elect the board that governs the entire process of decision making by the management.

Common stock yields much income over a given period of time, leading to an increase in the capital as it may be compared to any other form of investment. There is a cost incurred in this capital growth since the whole investment is risky.

In an occasion where the company suffers greatly loses or runs bankrupt or even falls, the common shareholders may wait until other stakeholders like: business bondholders, creditors, and other executive shareholders are paid before they earn anything.

In other words, they risk losing their initial capital investment just in case the money is not enough to pay all the other stakeholders.

2. Preferred Stock

This is a kind of investment which represents a certain percentage of company ownership but has got no rights to vote. It may not be so for every company. In this case, investors are assured of a certain percentage of claims ever.

As we had seen earlier, this kind of investment has got an assurance of the claim and not as it is with the common stock investment. In common stock, the dividends are varied and never guaranteed.

To add on that, in the event of company collapsing, these shareholders are given priority after the creditors over the common stock investors. As for the case of preferred stock, their shares can be bought back by the company in an effort to increase their premium.

So we say that their stock is callable. Because of this reason, most people consider the preferred stock as debt as opposed to equity. Preferred stocks shares can be well placed or rated as the intermediary between the common stock shares and the bonds.

Reasons Why Companies Sell Shares

Every company needs money to run its affairs and activities. There are very many avenues which are used to raise the company's capital. One of the ways is through the selling of company shares or stocks.

It can also decide to borrow from its creditors depending on some factors in place.

Whichever way, however, has its advantages and disadvantages. Depending on the nature of ownership that the company owner(s) would wish to have, that will dictate the course of action.

For full ownership, they may go in for loans and for the case of corporate ownership; they may decide to sell off the shares.

If the company lacks funds, it is impossible to run its affairs or production. Sometimes getting money lenders becomes a big hurdle, and that explains why companies go in for share selling. This method has got its relative advantages as we will be looking at them in a short while.

1. The Company Will Realize Quick Capital

This should come first because it is the very key reason why any company would opt to sell off shares. By selling off shares, the company gets working capital within a short span. In addition, there are no fixed conditions and or complications when it comes to repayment of the shares as with loans.

A shareholder will always receive claims as a way of payment whenever the company makes its profits from the increase in the stock prices. In the same way, shares can be translated into equity in the case where there is a merge.

2. Attraction Of More Investors

By selling off shares, many people may be attracted to the company and more especially in what the company produces or offers to the market. Shares are sold through several mechanisms like through newspapers, social medial, air, and many others.

This creates much attention to potential investors who go for the shares. These shares, in the long run, increase the capital for the company. We can equate the increase in the number of customers with the number of shares sold to the public, thus an increase in the market.

As the market increases, investors also offer oversight to the daily operations of the company.

3. Limiting Of Excessive Debt

Loans are debts. If a company goes for a loan to facilitate its events, the debt literally increases. The way this debt is to be paid must be discussed and agreed upon by the individual partners or stakeholders and must be paid promptly whether the company sails through or dwindles down.

There is no flexibility in the repayment of the borrowed loans as compared to the shares. Recall that interests must be paid regardless of the company status in terms of profitability. In the case where the company is running on less capital, the lenders may not wish to reconsider their initial agreement.

Chapter 2: Options Trading Basics

It is quite easy to understand and appreciate the reason why most investors go in for stock trade. Trading in stock is very simple to perform; hence, good profits are easily realized. This makes other financial instruments not popular or likable as stock trading is.

On the contrary, options do offer a great alternative to stocks. They are less costly as compared to stock. As well, they offer higher leverage in terms of risk reduction and profit.

In general, the buyer of an option has the right to buy the underlying stock as the seller is obligated to release the stock at a specific price and date too.

There are people who believe that trading options are a complicated procedure. This is not so; options have greater weight as compared to what stocks can offer. This is evidenced by the various types of options trading available and how they are conducted as we will be covering below.

Types of Options Trading

There are various ways in which options are traded. These types have their own merits as well as demerits. In this case, you will explore the different types of options trading as well as their merits.

Basically, as you trade in options, you will find two basic types: the put and the call options. The type of option that you will choose entirely depends on the type of trade you wish to do, either buying or selling.

In brief, you can say that an option is basically an inventory on a price. When you buy an option, you buy a right too. This does not mean that you commit yourself to buy the underlying asset until the expiration date is reached.

Call Option

This type of trading offers the buyer the right to acquire the underlying asset. It is ever 'in the money' when the stock value escalates above the strike price. Investors buy call options with an expectation that the value of the underlying security will go up in value before the expiration date.

If it happens so, you will definitely exercise the option at a profit. Those traders that buy call options are referred to as holders. They may decide to sell the purchased options as soon in order to make a profit. The profit of each call option is equivalent to the value of the underlying security less the transaction fees, strike price as well as the premium of the option.

The difference in the above calculation is what is referred to as the intrinsic value. When the price of an underlying asset does not reach high above the strike price, the investor incurs a loss. The amount lost will be equal to the option's premium.

The reason why most people purchase options rather than going in directly for the underlying assets is that options offer more leverage as compared to normal assets.

There are three things which constitute options- strike price, premium and the exercise or expiration date. When you hear of the premium, it refers to the amount you have to pay for you to get an option. It is always in cash form. An option takes care of one hundred shares of stock.

Example: Assume you are purchasing a call option for a certain stock at $53 as the strike price. The premium is $5 with one month as the expiration date. You will have to pay $5 to the seller for the option except if you decide to exercise it.

Put Option

A put option provides you with the right to sell an asset at a specific cost and expiration date. This option can be used on a good number of underlying assets which include indexes, commodities, stocks, and currencies. The price at which a trade makes his sale of an option is usually referred to as strike price.

You can only generate profit from a put option when the value of the underlying asset goes down lower than the strike price. On the other hand, you stand to lose it when the value moves up above the strike price.

As time elapses, the value of a put also drops. This can be well explained in relation to the expiration date. As it nears, the probability of the underlying asset drop lower than the strike price reduces.

Intrinsic value

The intrinsic value of a put option is the difference between the stock price and the strike price (Stock price-strike price). The intrinsic value is greatly affected as the option loses its time value. A put option is said to be 'in the money' when it has a positive intrinsic value and out of the money if the intrinsic value is negative.

When trading put options, you do not need to wait for the expiration date to exercise an option. As the price of the underlying asset changes, the premium also changes to reflect the movement of the prices. You can, therefore, exercise your option at any time in an attempt to prevent more losses or recover part of the premium in case the cycle works against you.

You can also exercise your put option when there is a possibility of the option expiring worthless. If the stock price approaches the strike price and seems to be moving further down, you can exercise it to prevent incurring huge losses. In this case, the profit or loss made will be obtained by subtracting the premium paid from the premium collected.

Advantages of Trading with Options

Options trading have been in existence for quite a number of years now. Over his great period, options trading have been viewed as a very risky investment which could only be handled by Forex trading experts.

However, there are strengths that come with this type of trade. We will look at some of them briefly.

Cost Efficiency

There is a great possibility of achieving much from options trade by just applying very little capital. This is the reason why most investors would wish to trade in options alongside other businesses or stock trading.

Beginners who start small also benefit from the trade if they equip themselves with the rightful information and strategies. You could get an option position similar to a stock position at relatively limited costs. For example, suppose you wish to purchase one hundred shares of stock selling at $60 per share. You will require $6000 to make the purchase.

On the other hand, if you wish to get two options going at #15 each, you will only need #3000 as premium for the same amount of stock since each call option stands for 100 shares. Therefore, you will be able to save the extra #3000 which you can use to invest anywhere else or maybe make interest out of it by leaving it in the bank as savings.

Cost efficiency is an advantage which most investors leverage to create large incomes from their capital. This benefit is just unique for put option and is rear in other forms of financial investments.

By taking a position on an underlying security, you will be enabled to cut down the investment costs, therefore, make some profits at the same time.

Passive Income

Some strategies that are applied in an options trade will allow you to make a monthly income from the same. The covered call options, in this case, will give you an opportunity to purchase stocks as you earn some premium through the sale of calls from the stock to other traders. You will retain your stock as you make some profit by the way.

There Are Predefined Risks

The strategies used in options trading allow you to evaluate the maximum risk involved in each contract. This is a great advantage to options traders simply because you are able to anticipate your profits or loses beforehand. It will give you the confidence required in the trade since you would already have taken away the fear of the unknown.

By spreading your trades as well as adjusting the size of your strikes, you will be able to minimize potential losses. In the beginning, setting up risk management strategies is always very hard.

With time and as you acquaint yourself to the business; it becomes easy for you to come up with combined strategies that can help maximize opportunities to make more income.

As a trader, it is only the right but not the obligation for you to be in business. You must have understood well and clearly how you can make more profits by limiting the risks in the business.

At the expiry dates, when the cost of an option is not yet good, the buyer forfeits the right in this case, the premium thus allowing the contract to expire worthlessly.

In general, the option needs less financial equity as compared to other financial instruments. However much they are dependable than stock, the level of risk involved depends on how you trade. You may end up losing a lot and risking more if you are not very careful.

You can apply a stop-loss order to protect yourself from further loses beyond a certain level of your premium. This is an order which restricts the trade from moving beyond the indicated limit and may save you from getting further losses.

Let's say you purchase stock at $50 but do not want to lose more than 10% of this. You can place a $45 order to sell your option when the trade hits the $45 mark.

Options are known for their high returns. When they pay off, the profits are good.

Versatility

One great characteristic of options is the flexibility that comes with the trade. This feature gives you several opportunities to make money from the options market. Options are traded in the form of contracts that can give you either passive or active income, in several ways.

There are several strategies that you can use to make money from the options market. For instance, if you want to trade options on long-term, you can choose underlying stocks that have the potential of increasing in cost over time. If you are in the business on a short-term basis, you can get stocks that are able to give you regular returns.

Options and Time

With options, you do not have to watch the market all day to make a profit from a trade. Unlike other instruments that only use the buy and hold strategy, options allow you to spread your contracts across favorable price movements.

This is commonly referred to as out-of-the-money trading. In this strategy, the trader starts an options contract with the hope that the price will increase. If the probability of success is high, then the trader does not need to monitor the trade, especially if it is a long-term contract.

This strategy, however, does not work with aggressive trades with shorter expiration periods since there is not sufficient time for the prices to build up.

Components of an Option Contract

There are several constituents of any option contract that is opened for trading as we will explore briefly below.

Strike Price

The strike price is the specific cost or value of a specific financial product at any given time. It is also known as the agreed-upon price and represents the price of an option that the buyer and seller agree upon before the expiration date.

Once an options contract is initiated, the strike price remains constant regardless of the changes to the underlying stock.

Derivative

Generally, a derivative is a contract between parties that gets its value from an underlying asset. The parties involved in the contract must agree on the value of the asset. Options fall in the category of derivatives since they give you the right to buy or sell an underlying security. They may be derived from interest rates, bonds, currencies, stocks, and market indexes.

Underlying Security

The underlying security is what the option contract is derived from. It simply refers to the stock or asset that you trade your options with. The underlying asset or security is a vital component in the trade of options because it enables you to calculate the potential risk of an options contract.

Expiration Date

Refers to the date when the option expires. After this date, the option is no longer in existence and cannot be traded. As this date approaches, the time value of an option goes down, and its intrinsic value rises if it is beyond the strike price.

The expiration date is also known as the exercise date. Typically, options have expiration dates that may range from a few days to a few years.

Time Period

This is the difference between the start time and the expiration date.

Shares

Each option represents 100 shares of the underlying security or stock.

Several terms are often used when trading in options. These include terms like in-the-money and at-the-money. An option is in-the-money when it generates profit for the holder on the expiration date.

It is out-of-the-money when it generates a loss and at-the-money when it returns zero profit, zero loss. Other terms that define options are long and short. When you purchase an option, you are long in it, and when you sell an option, you are short on it.

A long call or put means that you have bought a call or put option. A short put or call means that you have sold off a call or put option.

Fundamentals of Option Pricing

Option prices are not in any way limited to the cost of the underlying stock.

As a trader, you may never predict an option's price until you come to an understanding of the elements which contribute to its value. The process involved in placing prices to options may be very complex, involving complex techniques, strategies, and process.

In options, every option value which you encounter is not an imaginary figure, but instead, it represents a series of evaluations as well as derivatives which are calculated by the use of financial models.

Intrinsic and Time Value Options

A premium, which is the price per share of an underlying stock, can be viewed in two's. That is time-bound and intrinsic bound values. Intrinsic value is the option's value that hasn't been lost on time decay already.

The Black Scholes Model

This is a model or formula that is used by the traders to value their investments. This model works by the generation of the value of an option in relation to the contract prices.

There are several variables that will be combined such as the cost of the underlying stock, the date of expiration, the volatility of the stock as well as the interest rates in order to come up with estimation in cost for the options.

Chapter 3: How to Begin Option Trading

Understand Options First

In the early chapters, we defined an option as a contract in which the investor has the right to acquire or dispose of the asset at a given price in a certain time frame yet he is not obligated to do that.

There are two main types of options: the call and put options. As for the call, an investor has the right of purchasing the option before the expiration date at a particular stipulated price. You could only purchase the asset if you have the projection of its price increase before the expiry date with the intention of getting it cheaply.

However, the put option is different. You buy the right to sell the asset with the motive that the price of the very asset may go down before the elapse of a given time. In brief, that's the way options are traded. This is just a summary of the whole process, even though in the real sense, the process is quite involving and can be risky as well.

Anyone who has the agenda of investing in a very risky enterprise should take time and study to know it well before venturing into it.

Learn To Know Options Well

You need to understand and appreciate that options are contracts and any laws pertaining to any contracts may apply. They allow the dealer to acquire underlying assets or securities for a strike price in a certain time frame called the term.

There could be a variation in the strike prices of the underlying asset as compared with the existing market price. It could either be lower or higher. Options control larger values of stock, and therefore they are rendered riskier due to their nature of expiration.

Beware of the Risks Involved

In most cases, options are bought to shield buyers from loses and with projections. The optimistic buyers have it that they will be able to dispose of them and get more profits before expiration dates.

On the other hand, you could purchase options as a cushion for other investments. In this case, what you may lose is the contract price; hence, you remain safe.

You Need To Understand the Basics of This Trade

There are two distinct types of this trade that you need to know before you select the one to invest in: Either the call or the put options. In a call, you have the right of purchasing, but no obligation, whereas the put is a right to sell but no obligation.

Learn To Speak the Options Language

There are various terminologies which you need to make familiar as you intend to join the business. You need to know and define the terms used in the business because you will have to use them at one time in the process. Terms like:

· Writer-a person selling of the option

· Holder-a person who buys the option

- Strike price- this is the price that the assets will be traded off or bought

- Expiry date-this is the date agreed upon by the trading parties to conduct the business after which; the contract loses its validity

Preparing for the Options Trade

Now that you have acquainted yourself to the various terminologies and other jargon and slogans of the business, you are now good to go. Let's now look at the practical way of joining the business in brief.

1. You need an account

If you can recall well as earlier discussed, you need an online account or any form of account from financial intermediaries say, brokers that will aid you in conducting the business.

The fact that options trading is online; it explains why you need an account to file in your business transactions. However, you could as well file your transactions traditionally with brokers.

The fact remains that you need to have some knowledge of how accounts are managed and used before you open one.

2. You Need Clearance by Relevant Agencies and Approval

There is no way you can begin to trade before you are fully approved by your brokerages. There are limits that are set for you based on the size of the account and the level of knowledge and experience in the field.

Every brokerage firm would wish that you understand the risk factors of the business before you enter the market. This is so because when you make loses, the firm may not be liable. Similarly, you need to understand the terms and conditions of service of the brokerage companies.

3. Learn To Know the Analysis

It is yet another critical factor to consider as you join the market. The fact that options are traded on a short-term basis, you need to be careful to observe the movement of the prices of the security in question for a sooner profit.

Technical analysis has to be made. You need to have the knowledge of conducting the analysis- a must. You need to know resistance, support levels, charts, and chart patterns, moving averages as well as learning to know the essence of volumes.

Setting off With the Trade

Up to this level, you must be ready to start doing something. We believe that at this point in time, you have taught yourself how the business works and that you have the necessary details and material needed to kick off. Let's begin by:

1. Paper

Work-Trading

Because this is a venture that requires the investment of your finances, you need to avoid assumptions and imagination. Go right down and begin exercising it on paper. You can use a spreadsheet or other software that can give you a platform for exercise.

Try to calculate your earnings for a period of time like three months; if you find that there is a profit being made, you can now go in for the real trade.

Recall: paperwork trade is a model trade and not the real trade, so you don't lose anything thus do not fear, just exercise as much as possible.

2. Apply limit-orders

You do not need to pay for options at the market price for reasons that the price at execution may still be high. Have your prices named with limit orders to hike your profits.

There is a great need to revisit your strategies here and there for this will allow you to discover other secrets to more profits.

As time goes by and now that you are in for the business, you will be required to continue exploring the challenges of the business by joining other forums online to learn new things. Explore new techniques, advances, tricks as well as other related information.

You can even reconsider the trading strategies for a change or a stop depending on the nature of the business trends. If you are interested in the future advancements, you can go deeper to gain more skills and knowledge that may enable you to sail deeper and deeper.

Chapter 4: Tools and Types of Trading Platforms

Definition of a Trading Platform

When you hear people talk of the trading platform, they simply refer to the software. This is an environment created and very conducive for trading. It is used for opening, closing as well as controlling the positions of the market via a financial pivot such as a broker.

They are the brokers who offer online trading to investors or business people. It is done at a fee or waived rates in return for the online accounts that are run or operated by the clients.

In a Nutshell

· A Platform for trading is simply a software tool that is responsible for controlling and running the market levels.

· This platform ranges from a simple screen for placing orders, especially for investors at entry-level to very complicated or more sophisticated kits that can be streamed live and has got charts and messages mainly for traders at an advanced level.

· It is good to observe some ethical considerations whenever selecting the tool and platform to apply to your trade-offs.

Trading Platform Basics

First and foremost, a 'trading-platform' is simply an online environment that helps traders and other investors to clip their trades there as they watch those online accounts via intermediaries.

On board, these platforms are interactive in nature. They offer features such as artificially intelligent quotes, tools for charting, news-feeds as well as research forms. There are, however, platforms that are already customized for some specified activities such as stock markets, currency markets or exchanges, options markets, and even futures markets.

Types of Platforms

There are mainly two types that exist and that are widely used around the world. They are:

i. Prop platforms

This type of platform is customized by brokers. It is only used to satisfy their own and specific interests. Mainly used by large or vast brokers who own big businesses or shares in companies? They are not accessed by the public in any case because of their nature of customization.

ii. Commercial platforms

The name is so suggestive already. This is a type that is targeted by the day traders or day investors. They are easy to use and have very supportive tools but not limited to newsfeeds plus statistical charts which show the trends in the current businesses.

These features help the investors in the information required for research purposes or investment reasons.

In most cases, brokerage-platforms provide sets of features that are similar in nature. This makes it very hard just to identify one in comparison with the other.

There are always factors to consider while trading in options which include but not limited to the commissions payable. You may find that at some point, brokerages maintain a standard rate of commission whereas others waiver it through some discounts.

Trading Option's Features

· Quality of research

· Mobile access

· Option tools

- "Option-specific" platform features

At some point in time, as the sophistication is arrived at, you will discover that some tools are easily accessible but limited to some few brokerages. This alone is possible to trigger you to shift from one to the other brokerage.

Another issue that can cause you to switch is the nature in which the platform is laid out. However, the way the platform is laid out is the owner's choice. As before said, there is a greater similarity in the way platforms are laid out across the structures or brokerages.

A margin account is required across every options trade. Based on the option's type that you wish to trade in, you must encounter four approval levels out of which the fourth being the most cumbersome for approval. You need to understand that all the option levels are similar in all brokerages.

How to Select a Trading Platform

Before you arrive at the best platform that best suits your trading needs, there are factors to consider in the selection process, depending on the level of your business or investment.

For instance: As for the case of day traders as well as short-lived traders, their interest may only be in low-level quotes as well as some charts which can help them in making decisions as opposed to option traders who need advanced tools which are strictly created to envisage options' strategies.

Another very crucial aspect that needs to be put into consideration when selecting the trading platform is the concept of the fee. For those who embrace scalping strategy, they will tend to go in for low payable platforms. In summary, most people prefer low fees, even if they involve some trade-offs.

Sometimes low payable platforms seem to be advantageous; however, they may not be most preferable because of their limited marketing features. You may discover that some platforms are mostly embraced and most believed in by some brokers who give credit to its users; however, to some others; it may be a point of lack of an alternative.

They may be offering only a certain specific platform and that you may be left with no other alternative since that is the best you can afford.

Another factor to consider when selecting the type of platform to use is the intermediary's reputation. What have others said or encountered with this intermediary? It is very important to do such an analysis. I give you some insight into the behavior of the broker.

To sum up, every platform has got its specific features which you need to consider for qualification to work with. The amount of money required of you to have as equity is a key factor to consider for your approval to different kinds of trading.

There are a series of trading platforms around the globe that are being used to carry out businesses, but we will consider just but key or major ones that are popularly used.

Ethical Considerations for an Options Trader

As an options trader, your worry is to make profits from your input. You need to watch out on the type of platform and or the brokerage that you go in for you to achieve the most out of your investment. Most platforms, as we shall see below offer full-time services to its customers except for a few.

Most advanced traders may find loopholes in some platforms or brokerages. This alone is able to cause them to switch to other brokerages in search of better services and facilities.

In most cases, most brokerages do offer most of the features that traders request for; however, none of them can offer all that is required on the market. Even if you are already investing with a given brokerage firm, you will be tasked to open up an account and undergo an approval process.

It should be easy for you to shift funds from a single account to the other within the same brokerage firm.

You need to choose a brokerage or trading platform based on the rates or commissions that are involved. Business people usually minimize costs but anticipate high returns. Such fees determine the nature of trade investments that will be received at any options trading platform.

Every trader has got varied skill levels, knowledge and trade strategies, and perhaps the needs. Sometimes trading options process can prove to be complicated, and as such, those joining should look for a platform which has got vast of educative material for guidance.

On the other hand, those already in the business should find advanced level features for research. When selecting brokers, every option trader must take in to account his style of trading and the possible features that can bring about great profits.

Therefore, you should consider platforms in the following criteria and select the one that best suits you, your needs, resources, pocket-friendly, and user-friendly. Choose brokers who are:

· Good for beginners

· Low in service cost

· Good for active-traders like professionals and foreign exchange traders

· Best in education and research

· Option trading best.

We have explored enough about the essentials of trading options platforms, and now we want to sink deeper into the real platforms and probably the companies that are offering such platforms.

The following are types of trading platforms that we have been introducing in the previous chapter.

1. Interactive Brokers Platform

This is the first and better-known platform around the world. It is well embraced by professionals for the features it offers and the low cost for maintenance of their accounts. Its vast features enable the professionals to access market across the globe.

It is possible to conduct trade on their web page. They have one of the most complicated structures used in pricing; as such, only active traders go for it. As opposed to 'thinkorswim,' this platform is not necessarily meant for options trading alone; however, many options traders love and use it.

2. Trade-Station Trading Platform

This is a type of platform that is customizable for a few stylish traders who would wish to run their trading exercises in a more advanced style using customized scripts and in a language that is easily understandable to them.

It is highly skewed to option business but not limited to it. It comes as applications that can be downloaded and used on phones and desktop environment. To option traders, it contains good entry-level pricing built-in mechanism which makes it likable.

One major disadvantage of trade-station platform is the aspect of complexity. It is such complex therefore not suitable to the less experienced. This is just but a drawback, but for options traders, one has to prove himself as a strong-investor.

3. TD-Ameri-Trade

This is a company in America which owns the trading platform referred to as 'thinkorswim.' This platform is available in terms of mobile applications and can also be downloaded to computer interfaces or screens and be used locally.

It is one of the most admired and widely used platforms that contain robust information about options trade. This is available and widely applicable to both investors and day traders in America.

This does not imply that it is the cheapest-platform for investment, rather the tools that it offers enables you to learn to trade easily with options.

4. Robinhood Trading Platform

In this platform, there is no commission payable to or by anyone. It began simply as an application on a mobile phone though it has grown to acquire a web user interface that can be accessed by many. It generates incomes from very many sources, especially the interests accrued on the money available in the accounts on board and also through the selling of order-flows basically to bigger brokers.

5. Charles Schwab Platform

This does not stand out as the other companies have proved; however, their platform is essential for the low option traders. If someone does wish to trade with the best strong and advanced platforms, he can opt for Schwab.

The challenge with the already mentioned platforms is the financial part of it. The commissions are high based on the service they offer and the goodwill of the companies.

This platform is still growing, and there are some lucrative features that are being created which may suit traders' needs as time goes by.

6. Ally Trade Invest

It is yet another platform that is greatly used by the option traders. It loved its simplicity. It is applicable to all devices because it is not yet customized. It is found in its ancient HTLM version 5 languages.

Another advantage is that it has got a very competitive pricing structure as well as discounts on information provision. These key features make the Ally invest a top-ranking platform. If you maintain a hundred thousand dollars per day in your account, you stand chances of being discounted. Very many investors if not all can afford this.

7. E-Trade

It is a very powerful options trading platform with very advanced features. As for this type, they have vast opportunities that are offered to traders ranging from options traders to non-option traders.

Option Trading Instruments

Options trading cannot move on or take effect without tools or instruments. These are foundations upon which the business is conducted. We will mention them briefly followed by the explanation of each of the tools or instruments at a later stage. There are two major instruments that are commonly referred to: Call and Put options.

Under the call option, we have the long call option and the short call option. In the same way, under the put options, we have the long put and the short put options that works uniquely but closely related.

These are further enhanced by other supportive tools that will be mentioned once and again, as long as you still work with options.

Strike Price

The strike price is the exact cost or value of a certain financial product at any time period. It is the price that is agreed upon and that it signifies an option's price which the purchaser or the writer may agree on before its date of expiry. At the initiation of a contract, the strike price won't change even if there are changes in the underlying stock.

It is a very crucial aspect in this business contract since the price of the option may go up beyond it, especially when the underlying asset price appreciates.

When selling an option, you will want the value of the option to stay below the strike price, but in the case where you are buying the option, you will wish that the value of the option goes beyond the strike price simply because you are interested in making a profit out of it.

Derivative

It is simply a contract between two parties, and it gains its value from an underlying asset. All the parties participating in the contract should have an understanding of the total value of the asset. Options are derivatives because they give someone the right of purchasing or selling of the underlying security.

Underlying Security

We derive an option contract from the underlying security. It is a stock that you trade your options with.

Expiration Date

Refers to the date when the option expires. After this date, the option is no longer in existence and cannot be traded. As this date approaches, the time value of an option goes down, and its intrinsic value rises if it is beyond the strike price. The expiration date is also known as the exercise date. Typically, options have expiration dates that may range from a few days to a few years.

Time Period

This is the difference between the start time and the expiration date.

Shares

Each option represents 100 shares of the underlying security or stock.

Several terms are often used when trading in options. These include terms like in-the-money and at-the-money. An option is in-the-money when it generates profit for the holder on the expiration date. It is out-of-the-money when it generates a loss and at-the-money when it returns zero profit, zero loss.

Other terms that define options are long and short. When you purchase an option, you are long in it, and when you sell an option, you are short on it. A long call or put means that you have bought a call or put option. A short put or call means that you have sold off a call or put option.

Chapter 5: Financial leverage

For you to understand well the meaning of financial leverage, we will try to break down the terminology and explain it in a very simpler yet most understandable format as possible.

You will be able to define and understand why leverage may turn out to be riskier, the pros of using leverage in options trading and the level at which you need to use leverage in business for better returns

Definition

Leverage comes from the word lever, which simply means a rod or bar that is used in science to aid in lifting loads. Actually, a lever makes work easier. Similarly, leverage is simply the advantage that is gained mechanically through the use of levers to lift loads.

It can be put diagrammatically as below:

Lever

Effort (A) load

Pivot

As you can see above, the lever is being used to lift the load as the effort is exerted on the load at point A over the pivot or the fulcrum. When the position of the pivot is altered, much effort is required to lift the load through the same distance.

In the same way, financially, leverage can be applied using the same logic and criteria — for example, the operations as well as financials. We will, therefore, have financial and operating leverage.

Therefore, leverage simply means the profit chances that prevail in the trade as a result of some basic inputs called costs. The nature of the costs is static.

This is the increased mechanism of achieving some objective; to increase the ability to apply standard-cost asset, in maximizing the profits for the investors.

When we talk about financial leverage, we simply refer to the association between what the company earns before taxes and other interests.

Why Leverage Is Referred To As a Risky Venture

With leverage, it is like a businessman balancing on the coin. As you know, it is hard to balance on a coin because of its nature of instability. Leveraging in business is as technical and difficult to predict just like gambling. You cannot predict the outcome; however;

such businesses are the most rewarding suppose you land on luck.

When the possibility of gaining more rewards goes high, there is a subsequent risk of initial investment and risk of getting equivalent loses. When dealing with brokerages, they will require that you keep your margin accounts to some standards.

Your securities and the cash will serve as collateral to everything you will have borrowed, that will tone down the broker's risk. This, in turn, increases your risk, suppose you over-borrow, and the position turns out to be a loss that means that you will have to lose whatever is on your account and as well be able to pay brokers' borrowed money.

How Leverage Is Used For The Benefit Of the Trader

a. Trading Stocks

This means that for every market position, you need to invest a certain amount of money. You could be having a little amount, yet you need more in order to stand up for a given position. Therefore you will be required to borrow some amount from the stockbrokers who give you money belonging to a certain stock.

Assume you lose the position at the end; it means that not only your money is lost, but that of the broker is also lost. You will be indebted to the broker still. Do you see how risky it could be at the end?

b. Trading Crypto

This sounds more different from the trading stock leverage. In this case, it is the lending market that is put to task. You will be allowed to borrow the currency that is crypto in nature, such as bitcoins through your brokerage or rather goes in for the exchange.

Suppose you do not own any bitcoins, to begin with, the leverage trading will be very appealing. The coins are highly marketable because they go up in value unpredictably and without any prior warning. In this case, you need to be very alert else you may end up losing a great deal.

Pros and Cons for Leverage Trading

Pros

i. More capital with less hustle

You only require having a certain percentage of the total capital for a position, and the rest of the capital will be given to you by the brokerages.

ii. Easy to invest

The fact that you do not need to have enough money on your account makes it easy for many to invest using leverage than it would have been with stocks or other options in general.

iii. No initial pain

The client or the investor does not need to lose much time and energy sourcing funds for the business. As long as you understand the procedures, rules, and regulations of the business, you are good to go.

iv. Easy to manage

What makes many people feel like losing the game of this business is the pain of looking for the capital and the subsequent hustle to ensure that you make profits. In this case, you are only required to monitor the trends and the way the shifting in the trends is affecting the market rather than physically toiling to get profits like in stocks markets.

Cons

a. It is unpredictable

It is not easy to tell when the net jackpot will be hit. The nature of the business is volatile, and therefore, it is not so easy to predict the outcome from the beginning. This makes the trader sick of anxiety for the time being until he hits the jackpot.

b. Permanent loses

There is double loss in the case the deal flops. This is because, on top of your initial investment, you also went ahead to obtain credit from the brokers who would want their money repaid as soon as the expiry date or time elapses or as soon as the business ends.

If the contract closes on a loss, both your capital and the borrowed amount are lost. You have the obligation of paying the debt as well as nursing the loss of your initial investment.

Trading Smarter With Options

By trading smarter, it does not mean working hard to realize more profits. This involves the aspect of research in your market and business and working around the clock for the better of the business. You employ the readily and easily available tools and time to get most out of them.

Advantages of Employing the Right Mindset

Work Out the Right Habits

For you to achieve much out of your trading game, you need to fine-tune your character and habits to suit the business. It becomes a big waste if you are not working up to standards of the business because of the limitations in you. You need to embrace the good habits and for the unnecessary ones, give them bye.

Use Time Wisely

In business, we say that time is money. The time you invest in business should be equivalent to the returns you get otherwise there is time wastage. You need to sophisticate your research procedures and trading strategies to cut off-screen time wastage.

Be Cool but Vigilant

Whenever there is a stress factor, you need to remain calm. Recollect your mind, assess the situation, and try to compare with other situations and allow yourself time to relax. Do you feel like panicking or stressed? Cool down and wait for the right moment for you to make decisions.

Decisions made in haste usually have negativities in the trading program. So, ensure that every decision made should result from a sober mind.

Risk Management in option Trade

Just like any other financial investment, there are various risks involved in options trading. For most investments, it is always assumed that the higher the returns, the higher the risks involved. This is not the case with the options business. Here, the risk-reward ratio is significantly balanced since it is possible to make high returns from small investments. The risk involved in the trade is minimal compared to the reward.

When it comes to trading options, various techniques are used, and each of them has a certain level of risk. The good thing is that as a trader, you get to choose the level of risk you want to take. For each options contract that you sign and the orders you place, you can easily make a balance to lower the risks involved.

The more you learn about the trade, the more you will understand how easy it is to overcome most of the risks. Your success in the business partly depends on this. However, you must understand that whatever risk is involved in options is quite low as compared to the risk of trading your stock or underlying securities directly. The only common risk with options is losing your initial deposit, also known as the premium.

If you control your contracts with accuracy, you can always make a profit from the trade. For example, if you own 1,000 shares of a certain company and you think that the prices may go down in future, you can get ten options and trade them at a profit instead of selling off your shares. This way, you will save your stock from declining market prices. Some long-term equity anticipation procedures allow you to do this for a period of up to two years.

Predefined Risks

The strategies used in options trading allow you to calculate the maximum risk involved in each contract. This is a great advantage to options traders because you are able to anticipate your profits or losses beforehand.

It gives you the confidence required in the trade since you would already have taken away the fear of the unknown. By spreading your trades and adjusting the size of your strikes, you will be able to minimize potential losses accordingly.

When starting up, setting up some risk management strategies can be difficult. As time goes by and you get familiar with the basics of trading, you will easily set up a combination of strategies to maximize every opportunity to make money.

By now, you have understood how options can limit your risks as you make unlimited profits. As a trader, you only have a right and not an obligation to engage in a trade. When the cost of an option is not good at expiration time, the buyer forfeits the right, in this case, the premium, allowing the contract to expire worthlessly.

Generally, options require less financial equity than other financial instruments. Although they are more dependable than stock, the level of risk involved depends on how you trade. If you are a careless trader, you will end up risking more, and losing a lot.

However, you can use the stop-loss order feature to prevent you from losing beyond a certain percentage of your premium. This order restricts the trade from going beyond the indicated limit and may save you from incurring big losses.

Let's say you purchase stock at $55 but do not want to lose more than 10% of this. You can place a $44 order to sell your option when the trade hits the $44 mark. Options are known for their high returns. When they pay off, the profits are good.

Avoid Leverage

As we all know that leveraging is borrowing shares from brokers to enable us to take up bigger positions hoping that in future we will gain more profits from these positions. Purchasing on-margin implies that you go in for a loan in order to fund your position. What you need is only a deposit for some shares, and then the rest is on loan. The problem comes in when the expectations are never met. You will be forced to return the borrowed money from your other savings.

How to Trade Smarter With Leverage

The following are tips that will help you to take up the trade in a smarter way to avoid losses and other inevitable.

Trade Patterns You Know Well

If you want to fail in one day, try exercising what you do not understand well.

It will be the biggest mistake that you will have ever made in the business.

You may have to learn every option business and other businesses as you could, but you need to master only one that can work well for you. If you do not merge with credit business, then leverage won't work well with you; thus, you need to shift the attention to other businesses.

In the same case, look for charts and patterns which are easy to understand and explain. Why waste yourself with patterns that will give you a headache and a hard time to appreciate.

You Need a Stock-Screener

It is hard to work in an analog-style. Today, on all trading platforms, there is software written to guide the user on how to maneuver in a real-time manner. It saves on time and helps locate information on relevant concepts of the trade.

The screener will help in searching for daily lows and highs, average gainers as well as related news.

Work at Escaping Losses

The main agenda of business is to make a profit. Sometimes you do not focus so much on the profits because they are inevitable; instead, you work around ensuring that you cut possible loses.

In the course of the trade, you may get worked up and make ugly decisions. Suppose you had predicted a profit and it turns out into a loss, do not lose balance, calm down and reassess the event as you think of the next action.

You can do this by establishing a concrete plan that will guide you in making concrete moves only. With this plan, you will have all the details of trades and possible maps.

Learn More Business through Steady Mentorship

You can learn many things by yourself; however, it could be so important if you had a mentor who is a professional that can teach you the basic skills before you take it all alone.

Think of this; it is better for you to seek for guidance from a seasoned mentor who would get you on track of business and leave you as you accelerate than waste a lot of time gambling and falling.

As you know, no one likes losing because business is all about your finances and losing the business means losing money and regretting the time wasted.

Education is the key for all successful people, including businessmen. If you wish to excel in trading, you must feed yourself with lots of business information. It is very important to have the necessary skills and knowledge before and even when you are in the business.

Never Go After Promoters of Stocks

It is one way of gaining customers for a given venture. All advertised business ventures do not turn out to be your best; however, promoters are out to convince you to go in for them. Recall: not all that glitters is gold.

You need to do your own evaluation and analysis of the venture that you would like to be part of. This is because promotes do not tell you the hidden shortcomings of the business; instead they paint them out as the best ever.

What you need to do is to find out through research the information related to the business you are entering.

Chapter 6: Technical Analysis

Technical analysis is a strategy of trading where investments and trading opportunities evaluation and identification is taken up by analysis of the trending statistics of the trade in the market. The analysts focus on how prices movement and the volume of stocks affects the business to know the entry and the exit.

The analysis's main focus is on the patterns of the progress of prices, the signals in the trade that tells the trader to enter or exit, the charting tools, and how they work. Realization of strength or weakness of securities is a primary focus for the trader

This analysis helps the trade know the entry and exit time.

Charles Dow in the 1800s coined this analysis. After Charles coming up with the Dow Theory, other researchers like William P, Robert, Hamilton Edson and John gave their ideas that helped form a strong basis of the theory. Technical analyses continued evolving and took encompassed different patterns and signals throughout the years of research.

The analysts in technical analysis believe that the history of a security's price swings is of much significance for it predicts the future price of the security. Technical analysis assumes that the price of a security alone shows the public information of the security and therefore its importance is to follow up the price movement.

While using technical analysis, you need to use the right approach to be able to understand the trade well. There are two different approaches to technical analysis, and these are the top-down technique and the bottom-up technique.

Top-Down Technique

This technique mostly applies to short term trades. The trend analysis starts from the longtime frames then they come down to the short time frame. The analysts here asses the economy globally before assessing the significant scale trends in the economies.

They determine the big scale trends within the economies which they think have the best investment opportunities. The analysts here always starts on a broader scale before narrowing down to what they believe as opportunities. They then evaluate the sectors that can take advantage of the trends of the security in the market and then they finally select the underlying assets in the sectors that are favorable.

Bottom-Up Technique

This method of analysis applies mostly in long time trades. The investors here analyze the trade by looking at different companies individually and then create a business of the company on the market basing on the company's characteristics. Most investors here are small scale investors.

They look at specific attributes of a company when building the portfolio for it. They mostly buy and hold for a long time while researching the markets to get the appropriate time to see. Despite the delay in releasing their held stocks, the risk of loss is low and the return over the period or the risk-adjusted returns go up.

Different traders also prefer using separate technical analysis. For instance, day traders mostly prefer trend lines and volume indicators. These help them make decisions about their entry and exit in the trade. On the other hand, the swing traders select the chart patterns and the technical indicators in their analysis. There is another group of investors, the developers of algorithms. These types of traders prefer using both the volume indicators and the technical indicators in their analysis to help them come up with decisions of the trade.

Support and resistance levels analysis helps a trader know when to enter or exit. A support level is reached when prices are expected to take an upward trend after touching the support line. While the resistance level is when the prices are expected to go down after reaching the resistance level. Investors should be keen when analyzing the support and resistance levels in any trade.

When a resistance level is hit, a sell signal is set off. The prices are not likely to go past this level. Traders should sell their securities at this level because eventually, the prices will start falling, which will give them loses if they still hold on their securities. However, when the prices move past the support and resistance level, the work of the levels becomes reversed. The new level reached by support level price breakthrough below it becomes the new resistance level. While when the prices breakthrough above the support level, then the resistance level reached becomes the new support level. Support and resistance technical analysis method are essential in all the trades. It helps the trader be on the right track of the market and know when to buy or sell to remain in the business.

Characteristics of Technical Analysis

- Technical analysis looks at the historical market data of securities that includes the prices movement of the security in the market and the volume of the trading.

- Technical analysis believes that the data acquired from the market is sufficient enough for the market itself is an indicator of the future prices and trends of the security. The analysis believes that the market price is a predictor.

- It Studies the patterns of security through mathematical analysis tools like trend lines, charts, support and resistance and many others.
- Believes chart patterns are likely to repeat themselves.
- Technical analysis studies the movement in the market and not the goods in the market.
- It believes that the market is never wrong.
- Technical analysis answers the question of what should you trade.

Technical Analysis Charts

Different analysts use different analytical charts in the analysis of the trade to help them make decisions concerning the business. Presentation of various charts can be done arithmetically or by use of logarithms. This presentation depends on the analyst's consideration of information importance. Many charts can be used in the technical analysis, but the main ones are the bar charts, the line charts, candlestick charts, point and charts and the Renko charts.

Bar Charts

These charts are also known as the open-high-low-close charts (OHLC). Bar charts representation consists of the rectangular bars that have proportional heights and length to the value being represented. In technical analysis, the bar charts have vertical lines. These series of lines show the scope of the prices within that time frame. By using bar charts, a trader can quickly discover the patterns of the prices and be able to make the decisions. The patterns in bar chart analysis consider all the prices; the open, high, low and close. The opening price is always represented by a horizontal line that looks like a dash on the left side. The closing price allocation is on the right side of the horizontal line.

During a rising period when prices are going up, and the closing price is higher than the opening price, the line representation on the bar chart is always shown in black color. Some analysts use a green line for this representation instead of a black one. However, when the period is falling, prices are going down, and the opening price is higher than the closing price, the line representing this will be in red. It signifies the danger in the traders because the losses will be incurred if the traders do not act fast.

Line Charts

Line charts, unlike the bar charts that have a series of lines, the line charts have a single line that runs from the right to the left connecting all the closing prices. The only representation in the line charts is the closing price which is put in a graph, and a single mark makes the representation. Line charts are popularly used by analysts to present and report a general view of the trade movements, including the current direction of the trade and the history of the trade.

This chart does not give much understanding of the trade analysis, especially in intra-day price changes. Most traders consider the closing price to be of more importance than the open, high or low prices in that a specific time frame. They believe that the closing price represents the final decision of all the people after the analysis. It is the ultimate value. Most of the traders depend upon this closing price value for a go-ahead in their trades.

Candlestick Charts

These charts are also known as the Japanese candlestick chart. These charts show the price changes of security; it shows the benchmark price of the underlying asset or derivative and the currency. This chart was named candlestick because the main parts of the chart that serve as prices resemble candlesticks.

The candlesticks have thick bodies and two lines running above and below them know as the upper shadow and the lower shadow. The top of the upper shadow represents high prices in the chart, while the bottom of the lower shadow represents the lower prices.

Candlesticks charts patterns which are a formation from the real body and their shadows are more suitable and effective in analysis of short term trades. For instance, if it is an analysis of an intraday trade, each candlestick will represent a minute or whichever time the analyst decides to use. If it is a month, each candlestick can represent a day. Significance of the candlesticks patterns is at the top and bottom of the trend. Patterns here show reversals in the trend of the prices of the trade. There is a red color representation on the broader part in the candlestick when the security moves near the closing price.

Some analysts use the black color to represent this. The green color is used for the security that is trailing towards the higher price. The difference of movement in the securities towards the low price or high prices is seen because there is a broader part of the candlestick between the closing price and the opening price. It is straightforward for a trader using candlestick in analysis to see the gaps in between the bodies.

Renko Charts

These chars are very different from other charts. They consider changes in the prices and ignore the volumes and the time of the trade. In these charts, bricks or blocks are used. The white or black bricks are used in Renko charts. You may find a Renko chart that the green or the red bricks have been used. Green blocks are put on the chart when the prices go beyond the prior high by a set determined amount. Redbrick is put on when the prices break lower than the previous price by a determined set amount. These charts can be used by both short term traders and longer-term traders. Nonetheless, a new block can only be placed under a criterion of price swings between the lows and the highs.

The volatility criteria under which a new block is placed will either be advantageous or disadvantageous to the trader. The blocks can be placed in a minute, a day or they may even take longer than a day because their placement is dependent on the market conditions. For long time frame traders, the brick placement that takes longer is more advantageous to them than the short time traders and vice versa. The Renko charts give the traders who want to identify the support and resistances a straightforward way of doing it.

Benefits of Technical Analysis

Trend Analysis

The technical analysis gives the traders and the investors the direction of the market. They can know the time the price move down and up, therefore enabling them to make a sale or a buy when the time comes. The chart analysis gives a prediction of the up, down and sideward tends.

Early Signal

Imagine getting an initial sign in life about everything that we do. Life would be so secure, more prosperous and perfect for everyone. The technical analysis gives an early signal to the traders and investor on when the time is right to invest. The correct entry or exit time for traders guarantee them good returns on their trades.

Entry and Exit points

Timing is very vital to any trader or investor. Poor timing can result in massive losses and the extinction of the trade. The technical analysis predicts the time for traders. It gives traders the upper hand to know when to make an entry in the trade or make an exit. Different indicators in technical analysis are used to help the traders have this advantage of timing on their trade. The candlesticks, Elliot wave, moving averages, chart patterns, trend lines and many others help calculate the entry and the exit time of the trade.

Adequate Information

All traders can use technical analysis and become successful. It is applicable by short term traders, swing traders and long term traders. Enough information is gotten from the chart patterns, and the traders can use it to their advantage to pursue their trades and get satisfying returns. More information like the trading psychology, market momentum, volatility, support and resistance and other information is just part of the vital information that the technical analysis provides.

Cheap and Quick

Technical analysis software is cheap, and some are free offers from different charting software companies. Technical analysis is fast in giving information about a particular trade or security. It is quick and reliable for the short term traders like the intraday trades who trade in one minute to thirty minutes. Candlestick charts can be used in this case.

How to Apply Technical Analysis

An analyst who wants to use technical analysis must understand the significant steps of application of the technique. There are five steps of how you can use the technical analysis technique.

Identify a Trend or Come Up With a Trading System

You will have to come up with a training system of your own. For example, a swing trader can decide to come up with MACD Crossover (Moving Average Convergence Divergence) strategy. He will plot his line chart looking at the MACD line and the signal line. He will watch out for the crossing of the MACD lines and the average lines. If these two lines cross each other, a signal line is formed. Most swing traders prefer a signal crossover than a zero crossover. In this strategy, a sale will occur when the MACD crossover line is below the signal line. When you see a cross over line cross the zero signal from below, this is a show of an upward trend. The emergence of a downward trend can occur when the MACD crossover line crosses from below.

Analyze the Matching trends

You must know which patterns suit the technical strategy you want to use. You cannot just apply any technical analysis strategy to any pattern for it will give you wrong results. For example, not all securities match the MACD crossover strategy.

Get the Right Account

You should have an account that corresponds with the securities you are trading in. The account should be reliable and easy to manage every time you want to analyze your securities future predictability.

Choose a Connection of How to Track and Monitor Trades

It is like a pension plan for a retiring person. A trader should secure his trade by having another relationship of tracking or following the business. For example, he can have a connecting account that monitors the price movements, of the deal so as he does not invest in darkness.

Search for Another Strategy That May Be Needed

For the implementation of the approach to be more productive, you can identify different other strategies that can be used to do the exact work. This alternative strategy will have a double advantage during your trading.

Chapter 7: Mindset, Controlling Your Emotions (Trading Psychology)

Trading psychology is the determination of how the mental state of a person and his emotions affects the failure or the success of in securities trading. Mental state and emotions influence the character of someone in a trade. You should understand that trading psychology is equally important like knowledge needed for the work, the skills required, the experience of the work and many other necessary characteristics in trading.

Trading in securities has many challenges, and your emotion is just one of the challenge or advantage of your trade. Emotions contribute either to the success of your trade or the failure of your trade. Human beings are emotional beings. Every person must master a way of dealing with his emotions so that they do not cloud his judgment and decision making. If a trader is emotionally affected negatively, he will not be able to make sound judgments concerning the trade. Alternatively, if the trader is positively emotional, his decisions concerning the trade will be an added advantage to his business.

There are different emotions that a trader can face in the market place are the significant emotional effects that affect the traders in the market place. These two psychological aspects influence a lot of decision marketing in traders. They obscure the judgment of the traders, and poor decisions are made under the influence of these two.

When you understand trading psychology well, you will realize that the most challenging work in trading is the trader working on his emotions. When a trader can work on his feelings, he will be able to control his feelings so as they do not affect his trade. To trade well, you must understand yourself well.

It is inside wisdom that lies within you that you need to apprehend and put it to practice. As a trader, you should know that trading is a stimulating experience and at the same time, a very personal one. There is no pretending in trading because it will hinder you to understand what is kept within you. You need to be yourself to realize the most extreme potential that is lying idle inside you.

Fear and greed that engulfs the trader prohibit him to see any importance of how his psychology affects the trade. The psychology of the trader represents 90% of the trade. Traders should look for means to solve their fears, instead of running away or ignoring them. Plunging into trading books, training, and other means will not solve the traders' problems.

Traders use different indicators, measurements and analysis techniques. Despite all the approaches above, the success of trading will always be minimized, unless they decide to accept the ugly truth that their fear and greed is an emotional hindrance to their trades.

No matter how good a management system and analysis techniques systems the traders have in the world, without working on their emotions that affect their trades, success is and will always be limited. A trader should work on his fears for him to be able to take risks that are well calculated and accepted. Running away and hiding behind other means is not a solution.

Fear

Fear is an essential thing in the survival of all human beings. Contrarily in trading, fear chains up the performance of a trader towards success. Fear is categorized into two groups, each bearing adverse effects on trading achievement.

Fear of failure

This fear makes the trader not risk anything. He is afraid of losing his money even without trying. He is fearful that if he invests his money, the trade will fail. He wants the trade to be perfect, and therefore he cannot risk finding out the result. His self-worth of perfectionism hinders him to go ahead and trade freely.

Fear of success

Most people do not understand this fear type because it seems unreasonable to them. Most traders wonder how one can fear success when success is what they are after, and this is the reason why they think the fear of success is unreasonable. Nonetheless, when a trader decides to give back his profits to the trade, he sabotages himself, and this is a clear indication that he is afraid of success.

If a trader does not find means of curbing his fear and other emotional wars, he is likely to have a lot of stress. This stress will affect his trade because of wrong decisions and judgments.

Greed

Different practices are very harmful to the success of any trade and greed is among the emotional ones damaging factors. The following are a few problems that are caused by greed in the trading environment;

Aggressive Risk Taking

The trader reaches a point whereby he wants quick, substantial returns and starts investing unreasonable vast amounts of the money in expectation of the profits. This action is a poor investment because of greed because one is likely to incur massive loses because of the greed in case the trade doesn't go the way it expected. It is a very reckless way of trading. A trader should be able to control his urge of reckless unreasonable, emotionally driven investments.

Lack of Ability to Know a Loss and a Profit

The realization of profits and losses are critical to any investment. Every trader aim is to know when he is making a loss or a profit. Greed makes it difficult for a trader to know where he stands. The unreasonable huge investments with the expectation of huge profits slow down the loss realization because the trader thinks that the huge investment will bring in more returns to cover the gap. In the end, more losses are incurred.

Overtrading

The greed of the trader makes him want more returns in a short period. Thus the trades excessively than his capital or as per the market requirement. His desire for more gains from the trade is so overpowering that he does not think clearly of the future of the trade. The trader here overlooks all the rules and the requirements of the trader for his focus is channeled n the huge profits returns. Greed is an emotion that brings about careless trading because it will eventually bring about irreparable loses.

Greed is sometimes confused with confidence and risk-taking, but it is not. It is more aggressive, and the traders need to control it because the overtrading brings about loose of control over the trade, which causes failure. Greed is mostly accompanied by excessive happiness that your business is performing well, so you decide to invest mainly. This is wrong, and your emotions should be controlled before they bring your trade to the knees.

Things that Distinguish Winning and Losing Traders in Option Trading

We discussed above that trading is a personal experience. It is among the own experiences that need time, concentration and sacrifice. Trading is like computers input and output. What you feed in is what you get. (GIGO) Garbage in garbage out. Trading results are a reflection of your doing. Attitude is a very vital element when it comes to trading. Your attitude can take you to a successful trading road or the road of a failure depending with how it is. A negative attitude is a determent of failure in your trade while your positive attitude is beneficial to your trade. In this case, the equity curve is evident. What you think of yourself is what will be mirrored to you in the curve.

Out-of-the-money options with a combination of sort time frames is a good investment. The capital to invest is always lower with huge returns. Before commencing on this trade, you should understand things that separate the winners and the losers in this trade. Two traders can still trade in this option, and one can win while the other trader can lose. The difference between the two traders is only one variable, for everything else is the same.

The difference in the thinking of the two traders brings out the difference in trade performance. The winning traders think different from the losing trader. This sign signifies that winning or losing in options trading is not in other variables apart from one; the psychology of the traders. The success or failure of the trade is all in their heads.

Realistic Expectations

In trading, every trader has expectations, but it takes realistic expectations for the trade to be successful. Winner traders' expectations are realistic. His goals are smart. He knows what he wants to achieve in a specific timeframe and is not influenced by anything else outside his goals. He does not think of getting richer faster by investing aimlessly. The realistic expectations of a winning trader are a show of his control over his emotions. His risk level rate is minimal risk. A winning trader does not commit careless mistakes during investment because his judgment of the market is straightforward.

On the other hand, losing traders have unrealistic expectations. Their urge for richness is high. They think that by overtrading and making a lot of leverages in the markets, they are likely to get more returns in a short period. The losing traders do not follow steps during trading for their judgment is clouded by the vast returns expectations. Timeframe matters a lot to them than risk minimization and technical analysis. With this mentality, the traders invest poorly without thinking clearly through the hopes and eventually, they are likely to incur massive losses.

Managing risk

Risk management in trading is essential. Winning traders are good at managing the risks. Their effective management of risks gives excellent profitable opportunities in the trade. In case of loss, they are well calculated for, and the winning traders can go on with the trade well because their emotions are under control and well separated from the trade. Winning traders will continue managing their risks well even if they earn more times or loose in a row. The looser traders always have a good start of risk management when starting the trade. They continue well until they get lost on the way. They lose their way and control after a series of winning or a series of losing.

The winner traders understand the importance of market trends in different time frames. These traders maintain their stand on risk management. The loser traders think that they might get more by overtrading to cover the losses incurred or to get more money faster. In by so doing, they suffer more loses. The winning option traders can only trade with the amount of capital they can afford to lose. On the other hand, the looser traders who overtrade and use up the amount that if they incur a loss, it will be too grievous that their trade will not survive.

Losing traders convince people that they can lose the money they invested comfortably, but the truth is, they are so much stressed about their investment. This emotional torture makes them commit more faults with expectations of getting their "comfortable investment" losses investment returns back. If the investment wins, they quickly reinvest without looking at the risk levels of the trade. This action is an inferior way of risk management. The bottom line is that the winning traders have control over their emotions. This control helps them manage the risks well and keep winning. The loser traders have no control of their feelings; that is why they can jump into another trade and invest without thinking of the risks because of excessive happiness from the prior winning.

Taking Profits

The strategies of profit-taking by winning traders are set. They are outlined well, and the winning traders know that the vital thing in trade is to manage the risks, then the profits will eventually be seen. The losing traders do the complete opposite of the winning traders. Their focus is on the enormous benefits without bearing in mind how to manage the risk levels in the trade.

In most cases, the losing trader's profits are minimal. The losing traders do not understand the risk to reward. They know the reward only and forget about the risks involved.

The winning traders understand the importance of having trust in your trade. They know that when you believe in your trade, your attitude will be positive, and the results will be positive. The market will be favorable because of your positive attitude, and the profits will be realized. When you do not believe in your trade or when you lose the trust you had at first on the way, the market will leave. They will see the confusion and the wrong decisions being made in your trade. Loses will be evident or stagnation will take place in certain stages of the business.

Trading Strategies

Trading strategies with emotional attachments are bound to fail. Winning traders know how to detach their emotions from the approach so that the procedures are adequate. Their trading strategies are not expensive and complicated. Complicated strategies will stress you up while trying to understand them. The valuable strategy will take a lot of money which might not be replaced if the trade does not turn out as planned. The winning traders are very patient with any strategy that they want to use. They are not hasty in going in any trade unless they have analyzed the strategy well and understood the risks involved. The losing traders are the total opposite of this. Their patience with the trading strategy is limited because they want substantial quick profits. They do not test the approach well before going into the trade. They do not analyze the risks well using the strategy before going into the business. As a result, the losing traders meet significant loses in their trades.

Traps to Avoid on Expiration Day

Close Your Trade Before Expiration

The closer the options are to the expiration date, the quicker their value is lost. When you wait until expiration day to make a sale or a buy, then you are likely to incur a loss. It is advisable to close your deals before expiry day for you to be comfortable to start a new trade.

Avoid Options to Buy a Stock

You should have goals in this business. Buy options but to have a stock. This idea is like a cover-up. When the options are not in use during their expiry period, you will be able to earn from the shares. You should buy the stock straight away and not buying the options to get the stock. When your stocks expire, you are required to pay the money. This is devastating for if you had bought stock instead of options, you will be getting the price rises and therefore the profits.

Know the Expiry Dates Of the European Stock

European stocks always expire on the third Thursday of every month while the American stocks expire on the third Friday. It is still good to know this to avoid the confusion and the losses during the expiry date.

Chapter 8: Options Trading Strategies For Beginners

Options trade is a contractual trade showing the rights to buy or sell an underlying asset at a specified amount in a specified period. There are two types of options. The call options and put options. The call options are the most common types of options. Call options give the mandate to the owner to buy a stock while the pout options give the seller the rights to sell the stock. Different put option strategies are discussed below;

Long Put

You can buy a put option after looking at the trends of the stock. When the trend shows that the stock prices are going to fall soon enough, you can purchase a long put option so that you await the sell to make the profit. When you own a put, to have a right to sell 100 shares of the underlying asset at a specified price but you are not obligated to the stock. The obligation is to the stock owner. The specified price that you sell at is called the strike price. You can trade in the put option until its expiry date. When this date is reached, the put becomes valueless, and its existence stops. Price in the put option rises when the price of the stock in the market goes below the strike price. When this time comes, you can sell your put option at the market price and get profits. If the prices of the stock in the market remain constant or do not go below the strike price, then you are in trouble. You will lose the amount you paid for the put option (the premium).

Protective Put or Married put

A married put strategy is reached an investor purchases the underlying asset as well as the put option equal to a specific number of shares, mostly 100 shares. The stockholder only has a right of selling the stock at the strike price. The investor buying the option and the stock simultaneously has an aim of managing the risk of any downward trend in the prices of the asset when it is still in his holding. You can say this strategy is more of like an insurance cover for the investor. When the risk is too high, and the prices are going down, he is covered.

This strategy is desirable and covers the traders back well during the price fall. This strategy also engages the investor in all the rice in prices of stocks if the gain more value. Therefore, the investor an advantage or trading both in options and stock, and there is a limit risk. The underlying asset in this strategy is well protected, especially when the short term prediction is bearish and long term prediction bearish. In as much as this strategy seems so perfect, there is a weakness in it. The investor will lose the premium that he purchased the option with if the prices do not fall. Therefore before the investor goes into this put option and stock purchase trade, he should analyze them so thoroughly. In so doing it will help him to know if he will get a win-win outcome or a win-loss outcome.

Bear Put Spread

This strategy is a strategy originating from the vertical spread. An investor trading using this strategy purchases the put option at a specific strike price and then later sells the same put option at a lower strike price. The options he is buying and selling at the strike price are always of the same stock, and they bear the same date of expiration. This strategy is very confusing to most investors reading it out when not in practice. You must be asking yourself why an investor will buy an option and sell it at a low price.

The reason why the investor sells the put option at a low strike price is when the trader is bearish. The trader's price expectation of the underlying asset is of a downward trend. He is expecting that as time goes, the underlying assets price will fall, and his losses and gains will be both secured. He will not have to suffer massive losses when using this strategy. The returns in this strategy will also be limited like loses are limited.

Buying and Selling Of Put Options

Buying puts and selling them should be clearly understood. By purchasing a put, you get the right to sell the security at a specified price .alternatively, when selling a put; you have the obligation of buying the security from the option buyer at a specified price. You should sell puts only if you are sure of the profit margins after the sale and the comfort of owning the stock at the specified amount. You should understand that by selling the put option, you will be assuming the obligation in case the security decides to sell it. You should put this into consideration if you want to make the profits in the put option trade. An example of a put option seller is below;

A stock company Z has eye-catching profits from its products. All the options investors and stock investors want to have a share of these profits. The company is trading at the $300 as stock price, and the price multiple is below 30. The current worth of this company is outstanding, and this is the reason for its fast growth. If your outlook on their stocks shortly is bullish, you can decide to acquire 100 shares at $30,000 inclusive of fees and the commissions. Alternatively, you can choose to put up one in February at $280 the put options that their expiry date takes two years from now. At $35. You should understand that the expiry day of the put option will be on the third Friday of February after two years from now with a price of $280.

When you have made up your mind to put up this option, you are in acceptance with the company that you will purchase 100 shares at $280 in February next year. You will not go against this contract. You must understand that company z will not allow you to buy shares at $ today because it is trading at $300 currently.

The only gains you will earn is the premium as you wait for February two years from now. After waiting the two years and the stock prices fall in February to $280, you will get your premium of $35 per share. However, if the prices do not decline, your put options will be valueless, and they will expire. You will still keep your premium of $3500 minus your commission for the period.

The bottom line is that, instead of buying 100 shares at $30000, you can decide to sell your put option to lower your total cost (net cost) to $28000 if the prices of the stocks fall to $280 per share. If you hit the expiry day and your put option is rendered worthless and valueless, you will have a $35 premium for each share. The profit is 12.5% of the purchase price. The risks are minimized when you sell the puts of the securities that you own.

Buying a Put

Trading in long puts is mostly confused with married puts. Married puts act as a protective gear to the declining prices in the stocks. They are the insurance covers of the investor in case the prices start falling. They help the investor limit the losses. Contrarily, an investor buys puts with the hope that the prices of the shares will decline. The investor here is not obligated to the underlying stock but has his rights only on the put option. The investor trading in the put option buys a put option to either open the position or close the position. Most of the brokers call it, buying to open.

Buying puts more advantages than writing them. You get more capital to invest when you have less (leverage), and you also get the upper hand of acquiring the stocks which have no buyer. For instance, if your broker cannot sell a company's stock because he does not have sufficient shares to give to people, then the puts come in. You will earn your profits from the non-saleable stock. You will benefit from this inconveniencing trade period.

Entry and Exit of Puts

Closing and opening positions in a put option at all the time is crucial. A trader should understand when the opening time is and the closing time. Sometimes it is good to wrap up the trade and exit, especially when there is a red flag in the trend of the business. To get in and out of the trade can be determined by different tools. You must first understand the put option trade well before you make your entry. You should have a plan of how you are going to enter the business and the following steps are going to help you understand if you can go in the trade or not;

- You should understand the risk involved. The level of risk to be incurred in a business is very vital in the success of the trade. You must calculate the risk before you buy your put or sell it.

- Analyze the return. You must have the objectives of what you want to achieve in the trade before making an entry. Going into the put option trade blindly will make you a loser trader.

- Define the risk-reward ratio. This definition is not hard if you have analyzed your risk and your reward. The ratio should be well calculated that you will comfortable to invest what you can afford to lose. You do not want to overtrade and incur massive losses. In such a case, emotions should be detached entirely from the trade so that the ratio works out as per the earlier plan.

- Calculate your exit time. It is always good to know when to get out after making an entry. Traders should not just wake up one day and decide to exit the trade. The consequences of this action will be severe. You must calculate your exit time well to know if you will get a profit or a loss. If a loss is predicted, you can always change the exit date as long as it does not go beyond the expiry day of the option rendering it worthless.

- Understand your position size. A good trader should know what he has to invest. Investing more will bring your trade down in case of a negative turn. Most of the traders assume this especially when they have winning streak series. They get carried away by the winning that they decide to invest more with the expectation of huge returns. In trading psychology this is greed. You are running the trade based on greed. The better you understand your limit of investment in the business, the happier and successful you will be.

- Specify your entry price. You have to set an entry price is comfortable for you. Trading in put option without knowing how much you to trade with are very dangerous. You will not be able to calculate the profits or losses at any given period.

There are only two order types that can tell the position of a put option. The two orders are the market order and the limit order.

Market Order

This order is a request by the put option trader to through the broker to buy or to sell the put option at the best price available in the market before expiration. This order is the best entry or exit method in the trade of puts or any other option. There is no bargaining in this order. The execution takes place immediately the best available price comes up.

Limit Order

A limit order is an order where an investor buys or sells the option at a specified price. There is a limit to when to sell or to buy. It could be at or lower or at, and higher price determined explicitly by the market. This order makes investors stay in line with the prices. It is like a control rule on the prices. The traders cannot go higher or lower than the set price range.

Most people find the trade of calls and put hard. The following tips will help you understand how to trade in the options trade to your advantage.

Interpret the Technical Analysis

Trading in stocks becomes a problem when you do not have the grasp of which strategy to use while trading. It will be very reckless of you to go into options trading when the stock trading is failing. You will first choose a strategy that will help you trade and get the profits. An approach with minimized risks and reasonable returns will help you trade well in options.

Research On The Company

Fundamental analysis of the company is essential. You must know what makes the company you want to trade with profits. You should look at the company strengths and weakness before you sign any options contracts. You do not want to buy with a company that seems losing a lot of money or that is using the wrong, illegal ways to get their profits. This will have a negative impact on your trade.

Know The Time

Timing is an aspect that affects so many trades, and in this case, it will affect your options trading if not well calculated. If you have done your technical analysis well and seen that the timing is exquisite, then trade. You should understand your expiry dates, and thus you need to put up your options or buy the options according to the appropriate time. Timing in options trading will help you get good returns.

Understand The Difference Between The Options

If a trader purchases an in-the-money option, he should understand that there is a significant value attached to the option in the contract. On the other hand, the out-the-money option is cheap, but this does not guarantee the stock price is moving further before reaching the strike price. It is useful for an option trader to understand the difference between the two and know with an option he can trade-in here. This will make his trading successful.

Understand Calls and Puts

A trader should have sufficient knowledge of calls and puts. He should understand what a call means and the profits and entry and exit time. The trader should also understand when to buy a put and the profits that can be gain after buying it. The predictability in the calls and puts should be well analyzed to keep the trader in the trade.

Buy Calls and Puts

A new trader in the options trade should be a buyer and not a seller. Selling needs a more advanced understanding of the options trade, and it is riskier. Buying the calls and puts is less risky because the money used is limited to your options in the trade.

There are mistakes that a trader should avoid when trading in options. The following errors are common, and they impact negatively on the trade causing losses:

- Do not sell both calls and puts.
- Don't complicate your trade. Some seminars teach so many things, but if you want to put all

these things in practice, like the straddles, bears and spreads, they will complicate your trade.

- Do not invest all your money on one option.
- Do not sell options if you do not have extensive knowledge about them.

Chapter 9: Stock Investing Trading Strategies for Beginners

Strategies for Investing in stocks

Stock trading needs a lot of understanding to stay in the trade and get the anticipated profits. The use of different strategies in stock trading helps the traders know when to invest and how to invest. The following strategies will help investors in trading with the stocks.

Value investing

Value investing strategy is an easy but yet hard strategy that traders employ. Most of the traders go for the stocks that they are unable to sell ultimately. In this strategy, the traders buy the undervalued stocks of the company. Experienced traders can smoothly go about this because they understand it well. They will buy stocks from the profiting companies that other traders think are undervalued when compared to the current market prices. The traders then wait until when the prices the market price moves to make their gains. The new traders in stock trading with limited knowledge about stocks may go for the wring stocks. They may go for the undervalued stocks, yes, but from a company that is not making a profit in the market. This gives a trade a hard time to sell the stocks.

When you use the value investing strategy for a long time, you will realize that it is more involving than you thought before. It is always good to control your psychology when using this strategy. The emotional torment of greed overpowers most traders employing this strategy. They all of a sudden, realize that they need more money faster because the undervalued stocks picked up the prices and gave them good returns. Most traders here decide to buy more underestimated stock believing that they will get more returns faster. This is an unsafe move because the prices may not even change, thus causing them significant losses. It is always good to be wise when employing this strategy. The traders using this strategy are advised to purchase their stocks from reliable companies that maintain their success.

Growth Stock investment Strategy

Traders using this strategy aim at increasing their capital. The traders invest in growth stocks. They buy stocks from a small company that they have analyzed and seen the potential of growth in prices of their stocks. This strategy works very well if well analyzed.

Buying stocks from a young company can bring excellent returns when the markets are favorable. Most traders using this strategy in stocks get huge profits but are exposed to high risks because the young companies have not been tried, and therefore anything can happen. The prices may not turn out as expected in the market hence incurring losses.

There are no specific companies that the growth investors go for stocks. They can look for the stocks even in the whole market as long as they find what is suitable. The traders using this strategy mostly go for the stocks in stock companies that are growing faster. They consider the technologies being used in those companies, the profits in the companies and then evaluate the gains they will get if they buy the stocks and sell. These traders also compare the dividends they will earn when they become stock owners.

The Fusion of Growth and Value Investing

Fusion investing is the investment by traders while combining the fundamental, technical and behavioral analysis without looking at the historical background of the stocks. The feelings of the investor and the underlying value of the trade are assimilated. Fusion Growth and value investing strategy, valuation analysis is done by a trader through calculations to help in the prediction of the future stock value. Through his calculations, he will look at the cash flow discounts offered in the trade of the stocks and use them to calculate the present value. The present value calculated will help in the future prediction of trade of the stocks.

A trader who does not calculate the present value of the stocks is likely to be carried away during the trade. He will overtrade or go for the wrong stocks that will come tumbling down. Most noise traders lose because they are carried away by a slight show of a win. They invest without valuing the stocks and in the end; they will incur enormous losses that will handicap them trade wisely.

In this investment strategy, the trader chooses shares from a share populace (group) that he believes have value. From the populace, the shares that the trader believes are more critical are chosen. Lastly, he selects the stocks that he believes to have the potential to continue moving in the required direction. These are the shares that have momentum. Selection of shares from share population and the selection of the fundamental share by the trader are made yearly, while the selection of the shares that have momentum is made monthly. This strategy tries to combine the traditional and behavioral models to get a powerful investment model.

Passive Index Investing

Passive index investing strategy is also called the buy-and-hold approach. The investors using these strategies invest their money in different stocks with the expectations of getting higher returns as per the investment. The investors here do not aim at benefiting quickly from the short term trades. They buy their stocks and hold. The traders believe that you can never know more than what the market holds. You cannot think smarter than the market itself.

Traders applying this strategy assimilate with the market trend. They do not sell their stocks or buy them before or after the market shows the potential to sell or buy characteristics. The investors here hold their stocks to limit the fees applicable to them during frequent trading. The main aim of passive investors is to make the profits widely. They are comfortable withholding on their stocks because they believe that the market's returns become positive over a long period.

Indicators of Investing Stock Strategies

There are different indicators of stocks that will help a trader understand the direction of the stock in the market and how to trade. Most traders use technical indicators so as they can get profits in a short period. Nonetheless, these technical indicators used by short term traders are also useful and vital to the long term traders. Different technical indicators are used when trading in the stock. The types of indicators used while stock trading are;

- Trend indicators. These indicators show the direction in which the market is moving. It shows when the market is taking a downward trend, and an upward trend or a sideways trend.

- Volatility Indicators. These indicators focus on the uncertainty in the market. The measure of this uncertainty is in standard deviation.

- The volume indicators. These indicators are good at showing the signals. They can point out any break out in the trend line or the crossing of the moving signals when they are in company in the market.

The indicators below help the trader understand what to do in stock trading;

Simple Moving Averages

The simple moving averages also denotes as SMA, are trend indicators. They show the direction the stocks are taking in the stock market. Simple moving averages indicator is convenient to use, and it is easy to calculate. When an analyst is computing using this indicator, he takes the simple averages of the closing stock of a specified period. Most short term traders use 10- day prices of stocks to calculate the SMA while the long term traders use the 100-day price or the 200-day prices in their computations. A signal is thrown in when the stock prices remain above for an extended period. The markets bully the stocks, and that is why it is called the bullish.

While using the simple moving averages indicator, the traders are advised to be very keen when making their entry or exit. A trader should make his purchase when the prices are going up and approaching the long term moving average. This will give him good prices when the selling time comes. A trader should also make sure that he sells his stocks when the prices start falling under the long term moving average. When the indicator starts showing that the prices are moving towards the long term indicator from the bottom, the trader can make a sell. But if the indicator shows that the prices have passed the long term moving average, the trader can now purchase his stock. For example AZ Company's stocks for over five periods are;

$22.80. $25.30, $26.70, $25.40 and $27.70.

The SMA here =

({$22.80+25.30+26.70+25.40+27.70}/5)

=$ 25.58

The closing stocks of AZ Company are;

$30.00, $25.30, $25.60, $24.50 and $27.50.

SMA =$26.25.

We have seen that long term trade has more days, this means this calculation can continue until you finish all the periods that you want to calculate.

Rate of Change

It is denoted as ROC. This indicator shows the momentum of the prices in the stock market. It shows how stock prices keep developing. The prices can take a different momentum depending on the market. Traders use a 14-day time frame to calculate the rate of change in the prices. Two percentages of varying periods are arrived at and compared to each other. The positive rate of change shows an entry signal in this indicator. It shows the prices will turn and pick the required trend. Traders can make their entry in the trade when this signal appears. A warning signal is flushed when the prices start going up while the rate of change remains the same. This trend is a signal that a reversal is on the way, and traders should make their exit.

RSI-RELATIVE STRENGTH INDEX

Right from its name, the relative strength index indicator shows the strength of the prices of the stocks in the market. Relative Strength Index analyzes prices as overbought and ready for collection when the indicator is above 70 and looks at prices as oversold and ready to bounce when the indicator is below 30. When the stock prices are 70 or above for a certain period or duration, it indicates the trend is up, however, when the prices are 30 or below, this sets an alarm of a downward trend. Traders should buy when prices are near oversold condition because the price is going up and the traders should sell near the overbought when the price is going down.

There is no fixed timing or surety for stock trading when this indicator is used. In long term stocks trade, a buy signal appears when the Relative Strength Index moves above 50 then reverse back. This shows a pullback in prices; therefore, a trader cannot buy until the end of the withdrawal. The time a pullback ends and the trend of prices is picked again, and a trader can now purchase the stocks. When the prices are moving in an upward direction, that's an uptrend, the Relative Strength Index is always less than 30 that is why a 50 is in preference. When the indicator shows the RSI move to 30 or below, traders should watch out because a significant reversal is coming. When the RSI goes beyond 50 and then back, it is safe and short term traders can now trade.

Moving Average Convergence Divergence

The moving average convergence Divergence is like an umbrella indicator. It is denoted as MACD. This MACD indicator shows the change in momentum in the market, the strength of the stocks, direction changes and time or duration of the stocks. Computation of the Moving Average Convergence Divergence is done by a collection of the MACD oscillator which helps in its calculation.

The MACD oscillator has three different series that aids in that calculation. Two series are different from each other, but one is the difference between the two. The

MACD series proper, the signal series, and the divergence series are the series that are used in the computation of the MACD. The divergence series is the difference between the MACD series proper and the signal or average series.

The MACD indicator monitors the MACD lines that are at zero in the histogram. If the MACD lines rest above zero for a reasonable time, this is a signal of an upward trend. If the Moving Average Convergence Divergence lines stay below zero for an extended period, the downward trend signal is shown. Traders who want to stay in business and make their purchases should enter when the MACD is above zero. On the other side, the sellers that have their stocks on hold should make a sale when the MACD is below zero.

There are other indicators that traders can use while stock trading to help him control his trade well. These additional indicators include the Bollinger Bands, which measures the trend of the business, the volatility of the market and momentum. Fibonacci Retracements is another indicator in the stock trading that shows the pattern of the stocks in the market. The Fibonacci retracement indicator has a golden ratio based on the series. The numbers that apply to the calculation in this indicator are 23.6%, 38.2%, and 61.8%.

Despite indicators use and strategies, some traders find it hard to trade in the stocks. Here are the tips for trading successfully in the stock trade;

Be Careful When Choosing a Trading Style

You must understand different types of stock, the profit margins, the time in there trading, the calculations and many other concepts before you start trading with it. You do not want to be confused in the middle of trading because of the poor choice of trading style. Poor choice of trading style is stressing, and you will incur more losses than gains.

Match Your Style of Trading With Your Life

Trading is a personal experience. If you are someone who cannot sit at your computer most of the time, they do not go anywhere near day trading. Day traders are mostly glued to their computers following up the trends of their trades. A trader who wants to succeed must lay a strategy that will bring success to his doorstep. You can always go for the long term trading if you are a person who cannot take intense pressure in the short term trades.

Select a Matching Broker

Just because you want to trade in stocks, you do not have to pick any broker. Make sure your broker keeps up to your speed. You do not need a slow broker for a day trade. This will bring a lot of chaos to the trade, and massive losses will be witnessed. You also need to understand the fees you are paying a broker before you pick him. The most expensive fee in stock trading brokerage is the day broker's fees.

Make Sure You Manage Your Risks Well

You can use the low risk to high reward strategy. When you control the risks of the trade by buying, selling or putting a stop loss to trade at expected times; this will help you get high rewards.

Other tips will make your stock investing successfully like;

- Ensuring that your methods of trading are compatible with all markets.
- Select the best stocks you want to trade-in.
- Know the time of selling your stocks
- Analyze your strengths. You should capitalize on your favorable factors.
- Have people who understand the stock trading and are successful in the trade.

Chapter 10: Tips and Tricks to Trade for a Living

Trading can be a challenging thing to do, especially when you do not have extensive knowledge about it. You cannot entirely depend on someone else while trading because you will not know if he is honest or dishonest. A lot of people before entering any trade, they always test the waters first before entering the investing in the trade. We have compiled several tips for you on how you can trade well and make a living.

Create a Trading Strategy

Most of the traders lose focus. They always rush for the trading strategy that worked successfully for other traders. Just because a strategy worked for another trader, it does not mean that it will work for you. Get your plan that you understand better. Let your objectives be stipulated when you want to invest in any trade. The goals clarity will put you on track, and thus your trading strategy will be well in use.

Learn Step By Step

Just like any other thing in life, you have to learn first before you start doing it correctly. For example, you must first go to school, learn to write the alphabets well before you know how to write other documents. You cannot just enter a trade and start investing colossal amount. This will be very reckless and dangerous. You will begin by investing small amounts of money before you understand how to invest the vast quantities. You must first learn the trading world carefully before you enter a trade. , when you have clearly understood the trade, you can now start rowing your boat. This will help you get your expected returns.

Control your emotions

Your mental state and emotions are very vital in what you trade-in. They either help in the success of your trade or pull the trade down. Your behavior is a reflection of your mental state and emotions. It is good to comprehend that your emotional health in trading is equally important just like the knowledge needed for the work, the skills required, and experience of the work. All the characteristics you portray in the trade are linked directly to your mental health.

Different emotions like anxiety, anger, short-tempered, attitude are just a few of the emotional challenges the trader faces. The major ones are fear and greed. If you want to earn a living through trading, you should be able to control your emotions. Understand your trigger and then remove it. If you do not work on your emotions, they will wear you down. Emotions influence many decisions in trading.

When you understand your emotions well and know how to control them as well, you will realize that the most difficult work in trading is working on your feelings. Emotional control will help you invest wisely and make other right decisions that will make your trade successful in earning you a living.

Stress Less

When trading avoids stress. It is a trade, and if you do not understand, you are free to ask. If you are losing money, stop for some time, retrace your steps and start again. You do not have to be perfect. Losing in a trade does not mean you will not win. Stop stressing over issues that are beyond your control in the trade for when you stress up, and your judgment will be impaired. You will want to invest more money or overtrade after a losing streak, with the expectation of getting considerable returns to cover loses. This is very wrong.

It is good to understand the influence of stress on your trade and control it or limit it. There are different ways of managing stress, and different people have different approaches. A stress management strategy like watching movies does not work on every stressed person. Ensure you use your appropriate ways to manage your stresses. So make sure you are stress-free when trading and things will fall in place and have your back in life.

Practice More

Practice in general life makes perfect. When you practice typing on a keyboard, you will realize as time goes by, you will be increasing your speed. In the end, you will see that your typing skills are perfect and you can even blind type for you know where all the keys are on the keyboard. This is not different in trading for a living. Practicing the trade will make you more perfect in the business. You can start by trading on demos until the time you feel you have mastered the concept well, and then you can go for the real thing. You do not want to gamble with your real money when you do not have an idea of the trade.

Psychology

This s the key to trading, and it will help you earn a living better through trading. Every trader thinks of trading in his psychological view and makes a decision concerning. No matter how many books, trading training and many other pieces of training a trader has gone through, a good trader will employ the wisdom of psychology in every decision he makes. Be it entering a trade or exiting a trade. When you understand your psychology well, it will help you get through rough paths of success in the trade. This psychology will also influence your decision making, which will help limit losses.

Be Patient enough

Patience is a virtue that most of the traders lack. If you want to earn a living through trading, you must be patient enough. Good thing comes to those who wait is not just a saying that suits a situation that needs patience, but it is a real exercise that needs to be upheld for successful trading. When you want to get huge returns quickly in the shortest time possible without considerations of the risk and the technical analysis, you are bound to lose more money. Lack of patience will make blur your judgment making you make wrong decisions.

Be Confident Enough To Risk

When going into a trade with expectations of success only, then you have to re-fix your thinking. Life itself is a risk that we take in our daily endeavors when we wake up and involve ourselves in different works. Trading is not different. You have to understand that when you are going in trade, there are two possibilities. One is a success, and the other one is a failure.

Most traders dwell on success so much that failure is overshadowed. As a result, when a loss is incurred, a trader is unable to handle it and can end up making wrong trading decisions. You should have a mindset of failure when trading. You must be confident enough to invest an amount that you know if that trade fails, you can still compose yourself and continue by investing another amount. Also, you should know that if the risked trade turns out well, then you will get good returns. There is no gain, without a risking.

Have a Good Rest

Trading can be very confusing, challenging and stressing at times. It is always good to take a break. Stay away from the trade, especially during stressful moments. The healthy you are more important than the stressed confused you while trading. A break gives you a clear view of the trade. What has happened in the business is evident, and you will know if the expectations were met or not. A break will also help you make better decisions if you lost your way in trading. You will have a broad focus on the trade after a break, and this is both good for your health and the business.

Continue Studying

Trading is like schooling. You should be able to learn more new things while trading. Learning different things in the course of trading will help you understand more on your trade. You will understand the pros and cons of the business. Continuous education while trading will also open more opportunities in the trade industry. For example, when trading in stocks, you will learn more about the options.

Later in the day when you have understood how options trade, you can decide to invest in the options which will give you more gains. In this case, an opportunity of options came by leaning thought the stocks trading. Studying will take a lot of your time, and it will also need your commitment and sacrifice, but in all this doing, the education will be worth it. Just like it is said, patience pays. Your patience in continuous learning will reward you.

Monitor the Trends

Trend monitoring is very vital for a trade to be successful. You need to know where the market is heading before you put in your money. If a trader does not follow the trends in the market, he will be committing a massive mistake. He is likely to incur significant loses that can send him out of the trade. Trends help the trader know what is going to happen in the market shortly and also shows the current state of the market. If you want your trade to be successful, make sure you follow the trends. Any ignorance is equal to pulling down the business with a smile on your face.

Have a Trading Plan

Most people think trading is like any gambling game. This is not true. You should look at trading as a game full of strategies. Strategies that will help you succeed in what you are doing. If you want to be successful in trade and earn a living from it, you must plan. Come up with your plan of trading. Know what you are going to implement so that your trade becomes a success. If coming up with an idea is hard, you can always seek advice from professionals or other traders that are successful in the field you want to pursue.

Understand the Analysis Tools

There are so many different analysis tools that help the trader chooses which trade to start or which direction to take in the business. Various tools can be used in analyzing the data but charts are more effective. It is very advantageous to understand how to analyze charts because charts always carry a lot of trading data. Knowing to analyze the charts thoroughly will equip you with more knowledge ion the trades. When you have enough knowledge of a specific trade, your decisions will upright, and the success of the business is assured.

Trade Analysis

It is good to analyze your trade. This gives the right way of monitoring it. It also helps you understand the trade patterns in the business and use them to your advantage. There are trade mistakes that need to be written down for remembrance to correct them and make sure you do not repeat them. When writing thus trade mistakes, make sure you are honest otherwise if you are not, you will end juggling things instead of correcting.

Follow the Trading Rules

Just like life, trade has rules too. Following the rules will help your business be successful. The major trading rules are four, and these rules will give you a clear mindset of making the right decisions that will ensure the success of the trade.

Focus on the price

You do not want to wake up and put any amount of money in the trade. You must first consider the price of the security you wish to trade-in. Price gives you an overview of how much you will earn when you invest and what the trend is.

Stay Liquid

Make sure that you are not stuck in a trade that is not selling. If all your money is tied up in business and it is taking long, it is very disadvantageous primarily when an opportunity arises. It is advisable to stay as liquid as possible.

Practice First

You have to practice the trade before you invest your money in it. Go for the demo accounts especially in stock trading before you embark on using the real money to trade.

Do Not Try To Out-Think the Market

This is the last basic rule in trading.

Do not go to the zones that are illogical. Your primary focus in trade is the identification of zones which have lost balance and then enter the trade or exit the trade to make profits. Sometimes losses may be met, but this should not change your thinking to try and do something out of the market draw board.

Chapter 11: Brokers

A broker is a person who receives orders from investors to buy or sell on their behalf. The brokers charge a fee called commission on the clients for selling or the buying on their behalf. Entities also play the brokerage role when they execute the orders of a sell or a buy from the clients. The firms charge clients commission for the services offered. Some people refer to brokers as agents. There are different types of brokers and are found in various kinds of settings. You should know them to understand which type of broker you need for your trade. All the brokers or agents act as the third person in the business.

Insurance Brokers

These are the brokers that work in different insurance companies. They ensure that best available insurance policies are sold to their clients. People mostly confuse the insurance broker and the agent. They have some similarities, but they are different from each other. Among the similarities of an agent and insurance is the commission earning. Both the agent and the broker earn a commission for the services they offer.

The agent and the insurance broker also share a similarity in settling the claims made by the customers. If a customer wants a particular policy, either an insurance broker or an agent can handle this claim. An insurance broker is not multifaceted in his work. His specialty lies in specific insurance type. Some insurance broker needs licenses to perform their duties; thus, they must go for training on the insurance work and get permits. The permits can be offered by the state associations or the Security Exchange Commission.

Real Estate Broker

Real Estate Broker is a person, either a human being or a firm that helps a seller to sell a property or properties. Real estate brokers are essential in their roles of selling the property, but their decision-making rights are limited. A real estate broker cannot make any decisions on behalf of the clients.

A real estate broker must understand the real estate laws and own a formal real estate brokerage license. If he does not have these two, he will have to attend a course and pass to get his license. Similar to the insurance brokers, the real estate broker also gets his license from the government associations. A broker is entitled to agents. These agents help the broker in making his sale as requested by the clients.

Roles

- Valuing the property and coming up with a market value at which the properties should be sold.
- Listing down the properties to sell.
- Marketing the property in different ways.
- Showing the property to potential buyers. For example, a client who wants to buy a house will be shown the house by the real estate broker.
- Advising on related matters to the clients.
- Giving all offers to the client that has hired him for consideration. If the client decline, the broker cannot do otherwise.
- Preparing all the paperwork on all the offers.
- Sorting the properties by considering the price ranges as desired by the buyer.
- Negotiating the prices with a buyer on the client's behalf (seller).
- Ensuring all the repairs on the properties is done.

- Ensuring that the property is safe and in case of any threat, by the permission of the seller, who is the client to the broker, the property can be moved to safety unless it is immovable. In such a case, the threat to the property can be eliminated.

- Giving help to the buyer from the start to the end of the property purchase. The broker will guide the buyer on where to sign and fulfill any other requirements until when the buyer acquires the property.

Stock Brokers

A stockbroker has brokerage accounts. Their primary role is to trade in stocks on behalf of the clients through these accounts. The stoke brokers like the other brokers charge a commission on the services offered. There is a fixed percentage of 15% of the trade that is charged. For example, if you hire a stock trader to trade in the stocks worth $60,000, this means the commission the broker will charge you is 15% of $60,000 which is equal to $9000. Unlike the insurance brokers and real estate brokers, the stockbrokers are divided into two types known as the full-service brokers and the discount brokers.

Full-Service Brokers

A full-service broker is a licensed person to deal in more roles in the trade apart from trading the stocks only. A full-service broker just as the name suggests is a wholesale. These brokers can compute taxes for clients, research and advice clients, plan for the retirement of the clients, give different opinions and tips on taxes, and many more other roles. Since these seemingly complicated services are offered to you as a client, they come at a fee. The commissions charged by the full-service brokers are higher than the discount brokers.

Discount brokers

Discount brokers who execute the orders of the client to make a sale or a buy. These stockbrokers offer their services at a lower commission rate than the full-service brokers. They give a discount on the commission because they do not spend a lot of time to close deals with the clients. Discount brokers do not deal with HNWI that have liquid assets of specified figures, and this is why their charges are lower. Unlike the full-service stockbrokers, the discount brokers do not advise how to invest in their clients. They also do not have a right to analyze a trade for the client. There work is to execute the orders given. Discount brokers deal in small amounts capital and mostly work online hence making them online brokers.

Roles of Stock Traders

Customer service

The stockbrokers must offer their service to the clients. They spend time going around looking for potential clients. Most of the offices receive the stockbrokers looking for clients. Sometimes the stockbrokers use emails and telephones in calling the clients. They make sure they give excellent satisfying services to their customers to maintain the trust and the continuity of the trade. Through the services they offer, they receive commissions as their reward.

Client Recruitment

In as much as stockbrokers work for big companies, they have to form their clientele. They come with their portfolios. They move from one place to another or make calls to potential clients to recruit them. The more the clients they recruit, the higher the commissions.

Disclosure of Information

Stockbrokers must be sincere in their dealings. They should give the client honest opinion and information concerning a trade to maintain trust. Lying to a client or exaggerating information is wrong and is likely to cause withdrawal from the business.

Advertisement of the Stocks

A stockbroker can advertise the stocks to get buyers for the seller quickly and earn his commission. Some stocks are believed to be undervalued, and therefore no one buys them. A stockbroker will look for strategies on how to advertise and market these stocks so that they get buyers.

Advising the Seller

A stock trader should advise the seller concerning the market trends, the success tips in the trade, the tax operations and any other information concerning the stock trade. However, it does not mean the seller must follow the advice given by the stockbroker. It is entirely the choice of a seller to either follow the information or not. On this note, a stockbroker cannot decide on behalf of the seller without any consultation.

Client Recommendation

A stock trader understands his clients well. He knows clients that have high-risk portfolios and those with low-risk portfolios. When advising which investment a client can go into, the stockbroker will recommend an investment that matches the risk level portfolio of the client. If he suggests otherwise, he puts the client at risk of losing his money.

Executing the trade

It is the primary role of the stock trader and any other trader. He has to make sure the order of the client is run. A buy and a sale are made on the client's behalf. Execution of trade can take place in different ways. It can be done electronically or manually. A stockbroker can go to the client's office and make a trade there, or it can be done through phone or emails and any other electronic means.

High-End Brokers

This is the type of people who first studies the market and then advises their clients on the timing before going into the trade. High-end brokers' work is very and broad and to carry it out well, and they have researchers. The researchers help them in researching market status and economic conditions. High-end brokers mostly deal with people that are on top ladders of the societal ladder. It means the fee also corresponds to the clients. The commission charged here is higher than the commissions charged by all the brokers.

Roles of High-End Brokers

Research

The brokers perform research on market trends and patterns on behalf of the client.

Advising

High-end brokers give investment advice to the client so that he can invest intelligently.

Recruitment

High-end brokers recruit their clients from the high top of the trade ladder.

Customer Service

The high-end brokers offer different services to clients which includes but not limited to, advice, research, graph and charts analysis e. t. c.

Trade Initiation

Kicking live the trade is the ultimate aim of any broker. Taking up a trade on clients request and getting commission after making a sale or a buy as per the order is the objective in the brokerage trade. So a high-end broker initiates the trade and takes it to the final point.

Online Brokers

Online brokers like the name suggests are the brokers that work through the internet. They look for information about the investment as ordered by the client and present it to them through the internet. The online brokers work through the websites. They create different brokerage accounts that they use to render their services to their clients. The online broker has different roles which include, advising the client on investment, analyzing the graphs and charts for the clients and executing the orders given by the client.

Roles of Online Brokers

Functions of an online broker are more similar to the duties of a discount broker.

Recruitment of Clients

Through different websites, an online broker recruits his clients by either emailing them or calling them. All the work is done through the internet help.

Marketing the Stocks

For an online broker to get the clients, he must first market his stocks. When people look at his websites and see eye-catching stocks, it will be easy for an online broker to recruit them.

Disclosing All the Offers

It is the role of an online broker to show the client all the offers offered for the stocks. Hiding some offers is dishonesty and affects the trust intensity between the broker and the client.

Customer Service

An online broker offers services of order execution and disclosure of offers. The services provided by the broker are what make him earn the commission.

Trade Execution

It is the duty of an online broker to initiate the trade. He must make a sell or a buy as stipulated in the order by the client.

How to Invest with Brokers

There different factors that guide you in investing with the brokers. When selecting a broker to invest with, make sure you use the required tools. These tools will help you in decision making, and you will be able to choose an efficient, intelligent and informed broker. When investing with this broker, you should look at the price of the fees. If the brokerage fee is too high, this means you have to change your broker or the trading style. Over time people invest with different traders.

Conclusion

Technical analysis assumes that the price of a security alone shows the public information of the security and therefore its importance is to follow up the price movement. While using technical analysis, you need to use the right approach to be able to understand the trade well. There are two different approaches to technical analysis, and these are the; the top-down technique and the bottom-up technique.

Different tools can be used in technical analysis and charts are one of the tools. Many analysts use various analytical charts in the interpretation of the trade to help them make decisions concerning the business. Presentation of different charts can be done arithmetically or using logarithms depending on the analysts' consideration of information importance. Many charts can be used in the technical analysis, but the main ones are the bar charts, the line charts, candlestick charts, and the point and charts.

In technical analysis, timing is to any trader. Poor timing can result in massive losses and the extinction of the trade. The technical analysis predicts the time for traders. It gives traders the upper hand to know when to make an entry in the trade or make an exit. Different indicators in technical analysis are used to help the traders have this advantage of timing on their trade. The candlesticks, Elliot wave, moving averages, chart patterns, trend lines and many others help calculate the entry and the exit time of the trade.

In as much as technical analysis is essential in trading, the mindset of a person plays a critical role. The psychology of a trader will either influence the trade positively or negatively. Trading psychology represents someone's character in the trade that is influenced by his mental state and emotions. Therefore every person must master a way of dealing with his feelings so that they do not cloud his judgment and decision making. If a trader is emotionally affected negatively, he will not be able to make sound judgments concerning the trade. Alternatively, if the trader is positively emotional, his decisions concerning the trade will be an added advantage to his business.

The mindset of a person distinguishes a winning trader from a losing trader, and different things bring about the distinction. Attitude is a very vital element when it comes to trading. Your attitude can take you to a successful trading road or the road of a failure depending with how it is. A negative attitude is a determent of failure in your trade while your positive attitude is beneficial to your trade. In this case, the equity curve is evident. What you think of yourself is what will be mirrored to you in the curve.

We have discussed put options and the strategies, their entry and exit time and the indicators involved. There different approaches, like the long put option married put and the bear put spread. We have looked at every strategy and how it works. Buying and selling puts can be confusing sometimes. Buying puts and selling them should be clearly understood. By purchasing a put, you get the right to sell the security at a specified price. Alternatively, when selling a put, you have the obligation of buying the security from the option buyer at a specified price. You should sell puts only if you are sure of the profit margins after the sale and the comfort of owning the stock at the specified price. You should understand that by selling the put option, you will be assuming the obligation in case the security decides to sell it.

When buying puts and selling them, it must be understood that timing is vital. The entry time and the exit time in the trade determine your losses or profits. Closing and opening positions in a put option at all the time is vital. A trader should understand when the opening time is and the closing time. Sometimes it is good to wrap up the trade and exit, especially when there is a red flag in the trend of the business. To get in and out of the trade can be determined by different tools. You must first understand the put option trade well before you make your entry.

Understanding puts and calls in trade are good, but first, you have to understand the stock trade itself. Stock trading needs a lot of understanding to stay in business and get the anticipated profits. The different use strategies in stock trading help the traders know when to invest and how to invest. Various strategies like the value investing approach, growth stock investment; Fusion growth and value investing and passive index investing are used.

While using these strategies, different indicators help signal a trader when to make a move in the trade. Different types of indicators show the volume, trend, direction and volatility while trading. Signs like the Fibonacci retracement, Relative strength index, the simple moving averages, the moving average convergence Divergence and many others are used to show the performance of the trade in the market.

A trader knowing how to analyze a trade using technical analysis and using other indicators with the application of different strategies does not guarantee success in the trade. Tips of successful trading must be employed to make sure your investment in business earns you a living. A trader should apply tips like;

Risk-taking confidence, stressing less, leaning step by step, exercising patience, being in control of his emotions, creating a market strategy, having a prior plan of the trade, practicing before going into the business and many others. In so doing the traders should also know the rules they should follow while trading to maintain the clear focus on the objectives of the trade.

In chapter 10, we discussed the brokers and looked at the definition, different types of the brokers like the insurance brokers, real estate brokers and the stockbrokers which have two classes. We also discussed the roles of the traders and how to invest with the brokers.

www.ingramcontent.com/pod-product-compliance
Lightning Source LLC
Chambersburg PA
CBHW070644220526
45466CB00001B/281